SUNDER'S FIASCO

A TWIST TO WORLD PEACE

SUNDER'S FIASCO

A TWIST TO WORLD PEACE

Bhakta Sunder Sharma

EXCELLER BOOKS®
A GLOBAL PRESS

Sunder's Fiasco

A Twist to World Peace

Cover by Tales Talks Walks

ISBN: 978-93-48892-01-0

First published in India in 2025 by Exceller Books,
An imprint of GE Group
Address: G1, Dream Apartment, Degree College Road, Belgharia,
Kolkata, 700056, India
www.excellerbooks.com

EXCELLER BOOKS®
A GLOBAL PRESS

Dedication

I lovingly dedicate this book to my late father Mr. Nirmal Chandra Sharma, whose timeless ideals continue to guide and shape my life.

Acknowledgement

I wish to thank all my students over the years, the teachers I have worked with, and every friend and family member who has stood with me on this journey of life. Special thanks to two English teachers at my school, Prantika Ghosh and Arunima Chanda, who have patiently read my manuscript, given feedback, and encouraged me to write. Also, thanks to my editor, Saheli Mitra, and her wonderful team at Tales Talks Walks for editing and designing my book. And finally, thanks to the Almighty for bringing my story to hundreds of readers!

Table of Contents

Foreword

'Sunder's Fiasco' is a tale of a visionary who longingly aspired to free the world from the tentacles of malice, prejudice and falsehood. He yearned to design an idyllic land – a land of Buddha, Ramakrishna Paramahansa where man would think, speak and act in unison, spreading love and happiness among the multitude.

The book exhibits the unrestrained vigour and unfathomable passion of an educator who dreamt of illuminating the world with the rays of hope, compassion and solidarity.

Bhakta Sunder Sharma's 'Sunder's Fiasco' is a mentor's clarion call to the youth – the movers and shapers of society to awaken, march forward and lead mankind to a tranquil land of eternal felicity.

In this age of tumult and turmoil, hunger and animality, rage and animosity, Sunder's Fiasco stands as a testament to the ultimate truth of life.

"Lead me from the unreal to the real
Lead me from darkness to light
Lead me from death to immortality."

Mrs. Debarati Sharma
Assistant Teacher
St. Joseph & Mary's School

Preface

I regard Charlie Chaplin as one of the greatest men in the world of Today, Tomorrow and of Yesterday. He died in 1977. Charles Chaplin was much ahead of his time. After going through his autobiography, I learnt partly about the man who had taken the world by storm with his humour and satire. Through his films, he transpired his philosophy and became so much a part of my everyday life and being, it felt like he was my next-door neighbour. I saw his films mostly on television. What a genius he was! I wish I could have met him. I used to write letters to him and instead of dropping them in the letter box, I tore them at night and threw them away. I never addressed him as Sir or Mr. Chaplin. Instead, I wrote 'My Dearest Charlie.'

I am a teacher. Teachers are no longer respected in a 'shopkeeper's world.' We have now turned into 'Catalysts' and 'Change Managers.' Charlie was fortunate, he did not have to witness the post 'Modern Times' where one has to tolerate crass jokes of elite jokers. A man without culture is a bad man. A civilization without culture is a nameless civilization. These days students are treated as customers and teachers have to behave like salespersons. The true essence of a student-teacher relationship has vanished that was once unique, like a mother-child relationship which cannot be defined or changed.

Today's world is ridden with power-hungry dictators and needs another Charlie Chaplin, a great teacher to change the mindset of warmongers. 'The Great Dictator' was produced by Chaplin when the entire world snuggled up to Hitler. Chaplin's far sightedness helped him create a path-breaking satire. It was a time when many Western countries along with Japan were being spruced up for destruction. Paranoiac devastators were all praise; But Charlie Chaplin was the only exception who had the courage to speak of evil through his subtle satire.

The Kid, The City Light, Modern Times, The Great Dictator, The Gold Rush, Limelight, Monsieur Verdouse, The Immigrant, The Circus, and A Dog's Life are some of his greatest movies. Every warmonger, ruthless person, including the members of dictatorial governments should see all his films to realise how wrong they are even today! Sunder's Fiasco follows this war-torn world where violence reigns and through letters written to Charlie Chaplin and also to students from their dear teacher, this book is an eye-opener for those who want to build a peaceful, loving and caring world for the children of tomorrow.

Chapter 1
My Letters to Charlie

1

The words come floating every night, piercing my brains, hitting my nerves and senses like the ominous truth wafting through the TV screen. That final speech of Charlie Chaplin as the Great Dictator is all so very true in present times. The bloody faces of children sitting amidst the ruins of war-torn Syria or the skeletal frame of a young boy looking for food on the streets of Somalia, the religious hatred playing dark shadows of riots and the war mongering world leaders threatening one another with dire nuclear wars pointing to the end of human civilisation, are all but a nightmare even today. Everyday thus, I feel like writing a letter to Charlie, only if he could have arrived in this world again and given a smashing hit movie, catching the bull by its horns and teaching the brutes of the world on how to work towards human survival. I flip in my dreams, destructive thoughts of yearning cut through my veins. I know I have to teach, for that's why I was born, I have to teach young minds how to survive, how to keep our civilisation moving ahead.

Yet those words of Chaplin keep coming back!

"I'm sorry, but I don't want to be an emperor. That's not my business. I don't want to rule or conquer anyone. I should like to help everyone - if possible - Jew, Gentile - black man - white. We all want to help one another. Human beings are like that. We want to live by each other's happiness - not by each other's misery. We don't want to hate and despise one another. In this world there is room for everyone. And the good earth is rich and can provide for everyone. The way of life can be free and beautiful, but we have lost the way.

Greed has poisoned men's souls, has barricaded the world with hate, has goose-stepped us into misery and bloodshed. We have developed speed, but we have shut ourselves in. Machinery that gives abundance has left us in want. Our knowledge has made us cynical. Our cleverness, hard and unkind. We think too much and feel too little. More than machinery we need humanity. More than cleverness we need kindness and gentleness. Without these qualities, life will be violent and all will be lost...

To those who can hear me, I say - do not despair. The misery that is now upon us is but the passing of greed - the bitterness of men who fear the way of human progress. The hate of men will pass, and dictators die, and the power they took from the people will return to the people. And so long as men die, liberty will never perish...

Soldiers! don't give yourselves to brutes - men who despise you - enslave you - who regiment your lives - tell you what to do - what to think and what to feel! Who drill you - diet you - treat you like cattle, use you as cannon fodder. Don't give yourselves to these unnatural men - machine men with machine minds and machine hearts! You are not machines! You are not cattle! You are men! You have the love of humanity in your hearts! You don't hate! Only the unloved hate - the unloved and the unnatural! Soldiers! Don't fight for slavery! Fight for liberty!"

The clock had struck the midnight hour. I woke from my delirious sleep and took a pen and paper. I had to write. I had to write to my nemesis Charlie, I had to tell him to wake from his grave, I had to tell him about my mother, about every hate, penury and hardship I suffered and the ones I challenged.

2

My Dear Charlie,

My mother will shortly breathe her last. She is languishing under a quack doctor and getting the cheapest treatment. Her condition is worse than an impoverished street beggar in the poorest country of the world, even an emaciated beggar in the 'City of Joy' looks better. All her sons are earning, two are government officers, yet mother suffers. My father is a pensioner, still my mother has none to serve her on her death bed. What about me? Couldn't I have done something for her?

Well, I am a father, a married man of forty-five. I am a constant dreamer, like you, I dream of a unified world, where humans will live in unity and harmony, without any ecological imbalance, terrorism, exploitation, war, genocide, bigotry or greed. But without a proper democracy in every country no unification is possible. Today's democracy is like a toy in the hands of super rich business magnets.

Every election in every country is a holocaust of money, paid by filthy rich business tycoons and collected by them from the public in the aftermath through price rise of essential commodities that these businessmen trade in. We must think alongside our posterity to improve the very essence of the health of democracy. It has to turn into a super democracy, a real democracy. And it can be done and it must be done. Unfortunately, even the largest democracy India is run at times by corrupt politicians, dons, mafias and goons.

Gone are those honest days after India won freedom in 1947. And why just India? Even democracy around the world is in deep peril. Look at Middle East and Arab nations, same story the world around. Democracy needs to be expedited by people, or else any kind of unification is well-nigh impossible. Only a super democracy shall give birth to a unified globe and united mankind and every nation needs to be part of this super journey to bring a world movement for unification of our planet.

As I finished the letter, sleep came over my taut nerves, as if speaking to Charlie helped me in a way to relax, to get over the pain that nudged my heart. But there would soon descend a terrible news that would rip my quiet world into a thousand pieces like a bomb that shatters a peaceful town.

It was 11th June 1998, a sweltering hot summer day, when in the wee hours of dawn, Anita, my mother's ayah, came to the 1st floor room where I was sleeping. She shouted: "Uncle come quick, *dida* is not breathing." I jumped out of bed, ran down fast, reached my mother's bedside praying that she was alive and Anita was mistaken. But she was dead, she would never breathe again, or speak, even groan, or sing again. The whole world around suddenly turned into one big vacuum. "Ma," I kept crying and calling her, only if she would respond once. But she was stone dead.

What followed was a journey of shattering memories and pain, the doctor wrote the death certificate, Ma was cremated, my father roamed the empty house like a helpless soul and kept saying to anyone who came: "This is a great loss for my children. Their mother was their only world of joy while I was the headmaster in their life, who could not be reached easily."

My mother was born and brought up in Rangoon, Burma (present day Myanmar). During World War II, my *Ranga dadu* saw his family off aboard 'Jalagapal,' the last ship from Burma.

He had to stay back in Burma as an Assistant Secretary under Anglo-Burma Government. Much later, he managed to reach Chandpur in Bangladesh after a treacherous journey through the forested Arakan Ranges for months. From there he was posted to Shimla and his family including my mother travelled with him to the viceroy's summer capital. My mother was lucky to have seen Gandhi, Nehru, Sardar Patel, Jinnah and many other political giants of India while they came for the Cabinet Mission in Shimla. But then again *Ranga dadu* was posted back to Rangoon and when my mother was married, my father journeyed all the way from Batajore (in Barisal, Bangladesh) to Rangoon to marry her on 22 May, 1948.

It was often difficult for me to fathom how an educated, urbanized, proud mother of mine reached a semi-rural, forested town of Batajore with my father! During World War II, my father was in the Air Force and moved from Lahore to Bangalore. But then he took a call, he decided to leave Airforce and chose his calling --- to be a village school headmaster. He joined as English teacher at Khepupara High School in South Barisal as his prime aim in life was to educate rural children. Both my parents faced indomitable poverty, but they held on to their principles and dreams and managed to successfully raise five children.

The loss of my mother came as a rude shock to him, a man who had all his life led his students with an iron hand. He was now completely alone and in his loneliness he would lament: "I spent my life with your mother for fifty years and nineteen days." He was a total abstainer and very proud of his own existence in the world. After my mother's death his personality became diametrically opposite. Every night he would wait for me, just to have a chat. All my brothers avoided him for his oft-unapproachable personality. He had an unflinching short temper and it all became more volatile from the day my mother passed on. In course of conversation regarding my mother, he would silently shed tears and try to change the topic immediately. I seldom found a more loving couple, though they suffered conflicts too. The only person my Baba cherished after my mother's absence was me. Despite being bedridden with diabetes, he would try to enliven his lost vitalities, did physical exercises, after treatment resorted to morning walk, wrote personal diaries regularly and listened to Indian classical music.

He called me 'Bhakta.' I lost him too one day, February 3, 2000. Baba died from a massive cardiac arrest. My God died old. I lost my Sphinx and I took up my pen, words flowed, a poem was wrote:

Sphinx- Thou art no more

Time laughs at civilization,
Sphinx laughs at time
How thou art not there my sphinx!
My dream shattered at thy sudden
lionised collapse
Thy demise hurled upon me as a gift
from infernal zone of eternity, the worst
boon on the very onset of the millenium.
I turned aback even 'Ozymandias of Egypt'
the mighty symbol of the pharos
collapsed in the stark desert of Arabia,
Despite, thy departure was incredible.
Thou art a history, thou art my song, my melody,
my courage ,my strength;
can there be no resurrection of thine
like that of the prophet from Nazareth?
Thou wast installed with the regal dignity
of most astounding lion,
Alas! I am left here alone, alone and only alone
in the silent sea of man.
I look at the sky, my sphinx not found
I search in the stars, in the sun, in the bottom of the Neptune's empire,
I trudged the Sahara, flew over the crumbling block of Giza,
My Sphinx is lost forever, forever and forever.
Hark, hark me the soul of colossus,
I must meet thee, embrace thee, kiss thy voluminous chest of
great patriarch after my own destruction.
(A mute calf of the deceased lion)
On the Epitaph of my father

3

The void created by my father's absence to some extent was filled by Henrietta and my love for my son and wife Tamosha. But who was Henrietta? Henrietta was attractive and had romantic eyes. She was married and I was hypnotized by her looks. Then there was another woman, Kanyakumari, a singer. Though Kanyakumari was not so enlightened as Henrietta, she loved me deeply and soon turned into a great friend and silent companion after my father's demise. Her flawless understanding of my father's personality is still a wonder to me. She inspired me to write, to dream, to compose, explore, discover the dormant fire seething within me. She probably overestimated me and allowed me to dream endlessly. She was just like her namesake 'Cape Comorin,' the last supporting rock at the southern tip of the Indian subcontinent. Kanyakumari loved the endless Indian Ocean and I too loved the endless waves. We travelled to this end point together and I told her: "India had far more astounding civilization than what history communicates," while standing atop the Vivekananda Rock and watching the sunset.

Kanyakumari asked, "Are you writing a book on India's classical heritage?"

"Yes, as a citizen of the world, every country is mine, Earth is my mother," I replied.

I had her right hand in my grip and I embraced her, while she held on to me tight. The sea was roaring, the sun was setting, and the crimson hues flooded the western horizon, the holy gong from the temple on the Vivekananda Rock resonated. Suddenly I felt afraid. I released her.

Was I wrong in letting my emotions flow? I dreamt of my posterity, dreamt of a unified world, united mankind, and an excellent Mother Earth and its burgeoning beauty. Then what was I doing here standing with Kanyakumari, exploiting her weakness? I felt myself a sinner without a sin. But there have been so much sins committed all along and so much still being committed! The horrific deaths in Hiroshima and Nagasaki and all the hecatombs and genocide that happened before and after, sectarianism, bigotry, fanaticism, insipid laws, rules and regulations, cowardice patriotism, warfare, violence and hatred!

Human sin is all pervasive – we have even destroyed Mother Earth. I find so much similarity between my mother and Mother Earth. We never gave importance to my mother's needs, we brothers were not unified, just like humans on this planet and we are neglecting every figment of life on this Planet, Mother Earth being the greatest mother for all living beings, the most romantic, most loving and the most dangerous lady of the universe.

Chapter 2
Love is Endless

1

It was a Thursday morning and I always considered Thursday mornings as worst in the midst of weekly drudgery. And why Charlie? Because I lost my mother on a Thursday. I lost my father on a Thursday. And when they were alive, I did not pay much heed to them. After their deaths, I became reckless without them in all respects. Like a mad street dog, I forgot my purpose in life, my career and paid attention to women like Henrietta. A deep void descended. I had to get out of it, I had to exhaust my energy somewhere. But I could not strike a steady relationship with any woman I loved. Henrietta was not trustworthy. I failed to nurture feelings for Kanyakumari. After my parents' death, these two infatuations turned to burdens and spoiled my freedom. Still a massive phoenix of hope for the Earth, the world and man kept me alive. I remembered the lives of great men like Lincoln, Gandhi, Mao, Che Guevera, but my illusion to be as great as them gradually vanished.

I was lost in the deep dark abyss of my mind. My infatuation for Henrietta reached astronomical proportions, I had no clue why her presence turned so powerful in the sea of my soul. I had nurtured an ambition since birth to be great, I tried to talk like a prophet. I had no idea how foolish I was! In my vacant and frustrated mind, memory of my parents' death along with an effort to keep Henrietta out of my conscious mind, created a whirlpool of emotions. I was married by then and I neither tried to improve my family ties, nor guide my only son to be successful in his future life. I learnt once upon a time as a student that 'something is better than nothing,' but now it felt 'Nothing is more powerful than Everything' and I kept drowning in that ocean of 'Nothingness.'

Since childhood I wished to be an important man, whose life story would be scripted in the pages of world history. My mother influenced me by talking about the life of Sri

Ramakrishna Paramhansa. I was then a student of Class I and lived in Dhaka. I began to follow Paramhansa's childhood, but very superficially. During my stay at Batajore in Barisal, my ambition kept changing like the ever-changing sea waves, like the rhythms of tide and ebb. My father was headmaster of the local High School and secretary of the primary section. My companions were extremely unpleasant. I learnt more slangs from them than my class lessons and got downright beating from my father. That too had little impact, the scolding and beating was so regular, that I took it as a daily routine and got accustomed to it.

Those were the days when my ambition was to become a spiritual prophet! My *baro mama* (eldest maternal uncle) influenced me by stating in specific terms the details and descriptions of a 'prophet'. Again, the foolish and artificial efforts became conspicuous. Meanwhile, India too was going through a political upheaval. Pandit Nehru died on 27th May, 1964 and the nation was shocked, disconcerted and silenced. Just like Ramakrishna, I had followed Nehru's life as well and his death triggered in me the wish to become a leader of the masses instead of becoming a prophet. My foolish sensibilities of boyhood kept changing goal posts. It was preposterous. But then, I was only a student of Class V and did not have the visions of a mature mind. I feel as I grew up, that immaturity never left me, my erratic dreams always failed to give me any fruit or result. Even my love life gave me no happiness. Kanyakumari's assessment about me was ridiculously Herculean while Henrietta failed to feel for me. Her ambition was very high where even eagles did not dare to soar. Henrietta could never be solace of my life, her feelings for me were not sufficient to help me out of the excruciating trauma that I had due to my parents' death. I was be-fooled by her. On the contrary, Kanyakumari shook my world in such a way that even the sky knew her feelings for me. It was so sudden and unpremeditated that I neither could assess nor fathom. I was again be-fooled seeing her sacrifice for me. Nobody loved me so maddeningly like her, but I felt I did not deserve it. Henrietta once told me, "You can't read me." In reality, I did not dare read her, lest I lost her. Mostly in life, I swam through an endless ocean of frustration, but always I felt and heard a dictation from my soul –

"Though much is taken, much abides; and though
We are not now that strength which in old days
Moved earth and heaven; that which we are, we are;
One equal temper of heroic hearts,
Made weak by time and fate, but strong in will
To strive, to seek, to find, and not to yield."

2

My mother used to say: "Never get exhausted for others," though she herself exhausted her life for us. My puritan father dangerously protested my scattered imaginations, my spontaneous thoughts. After my parents' death, the purpose of life got lost. Holidays turned dangerous for me, I kept searching for my father, in the lane opposite to my house, where he lived. On many evenings I searched for my mother, specially at the twilight hour, when the world would be enwrapped in the rays of a dying sunshine. I feel I even failed my only son. After my mother's death, I started listening to ghazals by Mehdi Hassan with a portrait of dead Shah Jahan in the Agra Fort, drawing by none other than the great artist Nandalal Bose in front of me. Both the portrait and the ghazals sent me to a world where only flood of symphony reigned. I was so much in a world of illusion that at times I felt the songs were sung by me, the portrait was drawn by me!

During my graduation and postgraduation from Ravishankar University of Raipur, I was in a fix. I was a student of English medium, but the classes in the Raipur college were taken in Hindi. I was trying to fulfil my father's dream of becoming an IAS officer. Not that I did not try, but failed twice. May be destiny had already scripted me to be a school teacher. I dragged the yoke of our lower middle-class family with my eldest brother. I had been running like a hungry leopard to earn money by giving tuitions from a very early age.

Meanwhile, when my future wife Tamosha's mother expired in a massive heart attack at Dehradun, she came down from Dehradun with her grandmother and youngest sister. She looked so sad and forlorn that without giving a second thought I decided to marry her. She was a very practical and calculative woman and my infatuation had no meaning in her practical world. I had so much fallen for her that I even went to Howrah Station to see her off as her family boarded the Doon Express to return. Charlie, do you know why people I love neglect me so much? Probably my remarkable poor knowledge of mathematics always misled me to calculate for correct solutions. I don't know how to proceed with this congenital heavy burden, all my life. After marriage, Tamosha accepted me like a mother accepts a prophet child. No, there is really none to share the harmonized madness in me. Nobody's feelings are akin to that of mine. In my tremendous dilemma, I waited for an angel, an Aphrodite, a Venus, an Urvashi to reach me individually, to be hijacked by any of them and swim across the colourful waves of celestial inundation.

Among every loss, my fancy to enjoy life in the long run was probably the only enigma that allowed me to struggle and survive. Sometimes in my sheer isolation I quoted from 'To a Skylark' of Shelley

We look before and after
And pine for what is naught
Our sincerest laughter
With some pain is fraught
Our sincerest songs are those that tell of saddest thought

Charlie my Dear, I was afraid that my fanciful world I was weaving in my imagination might crumble. So, I firmly held on to the principle:

'Astamasatgamaya, Mrittuma Amritangmaaya, Tamasama Jyotirgamaya'.

3

During my school days on the wheels of super imagination, I toured the world, worked in every high position, loved and had affairs with most remarkably beautiful ladies. My father came to my class once when I was in class VI. He asked me to pronounce in Victorian English, "Holland is the lowland of the world." I could not do it properly. Henceforth he took regular English lessons till I passed class X. A leadership camp was organized for a fortnight in the periphery of our school by Y.M.C.A. in DNK Refugee Project headed by Father Luther and Sadasiviya.

At the ending ceremony, Mr S Banerjee, the Superintendent of Education came from Kondegaon (M.P.), 150 miles away, to honour the chair of the guest-in chief. They gave speeches, but my father delivered the best. Everyone was all praise for his sophisticated English accent and extraordinary speech. Still, I failed to accept him as my role model. He did not earn much, he had a quick temper, an unfathomable pride. I loved, praised, and adored other higher-ranking officials, despite knowing my father in his knowledge was far superior to them. Unfortunately, that realization came only after I cremated my father.

People say mornings bring new hope, for me it was very different. They brought with them anxiety, burden of tensions and canker of survival. In school, I was afraid to watch my father's angry face in the morning. Both my parents had high hopes, they wanted me to be great, and both their wishes I could not fulfill. Failing my mother was a trauma to me. All her children turned average. During graduation, I returned to my father's place at Bastar. In Raipur, I was underestimated by everyone, as I neither had a good pair of shoes, nor a good shirt and not even a good trouser to wear. I grew long hippie style hair, got a bellbottom tailored along with a few modern shirts. In front of the mirror, I lost my original identity, my dreams, my idols and even my ideology.

In 1970, I passed the High School Certificate Examination and my father was then the headmaster. I somehow managed a second division and every member of my family were shocked, they expected much better result from me. I was the third boy in the class. I did not see my father's face, so full of agony before that day. Still, I failed to measure the flood of love and expectation he had for me. I was given a choice, either to go to Jagdalpur to complete my H. S. course or Mana Camp Boy's Hostel for refugee students. It had Bengali medium and my father's school also had Bengali medium. In 1969, Pranab Karmakar stood first in the High School Certificate Examination from Madhya Pradesh and again stood second in the Higher Secondary Examination. Arun Kumar Sood of Bhilai Steel Plant School stood first and Pranab, a refugee boy of Mana Camp Refugee Hostel stood second. So I decided to go to Mana Camp Boys' Hostel. My father for the first time in my life honoured my preference. My *mejda* accompanied me to Mana Camp and the bus journey was very tedious. We reached the bus stand late in the evening and it was raining. We both walked miles with the luggage on our heads, got drenched completely, reached the camp and the quarters of Bhabaranjan da or Mr B R Das, who was the ITI Instructor. He was my father's ex-student, and a staunch disciplinarian. Bhabaranjan Das passed Matriculation in 1953 (the very year I was born) with 1st Division, securing letter marks in Mathematics from Kachhipara High School of Barisal.

At the time of my birth, my father was out of station. I was born on a December morning. The midwife was a Moslem lady, a quack attendant maid from the village. My mother was forced by her to go to the pond and she was bathed within one hour and a half of my birth. She was born and brought up in Rangoon and Shimla. During her stay in Rangoon Mrs Dicory was her English teacher. She seldom stood second in her life. The diabolic World War II changed the flow of her destiny along with thousands of others and turned her to a housewife raising her children in a remote location with all the hardships she had to endure and suffer! My mother will never come back. She was my only oasis in the desert of life. In crisis, in frustration, while excited, when everything in the world turned negative, agonizing, when I was nervous during any exam, she was always there like a beacon of hope, shining through the darkness. Her health started failing from the time I was crossing thirty. She gradually lost her lustre, confidence, importance and finally in the last years of her life she lost her original personality. She became totally different from what she once used to be! She used to be pleasant, soothing, powerful, sometimes stubborn and sentimental. She seldom lost her temper with her children. If she did, she would make up within the shortest period. She could not tolerate gloomy faces of her five children.

Anyway, Bhabaranjan Das was annoyed seeing us, as we reached without prior intimation. He was a bachelor. I was allowed by Mr S. P. Nanda, the chief camp commandant, to be in the hostel. Almost seven hundred students were boarders and food was always limited. I was one among the thirty-seven boys in the dormitory. Toilets were not given auspicious visits by the sweepers. We went to the open ground opposite Mana Camp Government Hospital to respond to greater call of nature. One noon, being blinded with hunger, I gobbled up my meal, though it was tasteless as usual, while I felt a big stone in my mouth. It was not a stone, but a big nail of a toe. I threw it away and ate. I never left my parents, my family before, for such a long period of time. I really missed my mother and would weep alone. Without her, my days in the hostel were full of trauma. I lost my over dominating father, my headmaster and my mentor just within a tenure of one year and a half. I lost their world forever and breathed my days in a world, very likely that of my own.

I expected and desired for a repose, an oasis, a solace. I went to Henrietta but she was selfish. Kanyakumari tried to soothe my nerves, but her effort to love me was like a rich moody lady's love for her dearest pet. To a great extent my only child and my spouse were the only solace to forget and envelop the burning conflagration for my parents' demise. And then there was my most bosom friend, my only nephew Samrat Shankar Roy.

4

My life at Mana Camp Hostel was incredibly dangerous. Many classmates and roommates liked me, but I was hated by most students who were taught by my father in school. The chief camp commandant did not allow students to go home during the Pujas, as the session started much later than the fixed schedule. I went to the hostel super, Mr. Mahato, cried and managed to reach my family, crossing 150 miles. My sir, Rakhal Raj Chakraborty was awaiting me at the bus stand. My mother, my only sister, my loving plump youngest brother and my over dominating father got ecstatic, on seeing me after two months. I loved my home though we had no electricity, my hostel in the refugee camp however did.

My Puja holidays went well and time for my departure arrived. I packed my scant luggage and left for my hostel. I appeared for the H.S. examination in 1971 from the Higher Secondary board of Bhopal and passed in first division securing 63.3% marks. It was also the time when Calcutta and entire West Bengal was burning from the terrorizing Naxal Movement. Meanwhile, in East Pakistan, Bangabandhu Mujibur Rahman launched 'Bhasha Aandolan' (Liberation Movement of Bangladesh). It was against the Government of Pakistan, ran by Marshal Yahya Khan and Zulfikar Ali Bhutto. The Naxalbari Movement started by Charu Mazumder, Kanu Sanyal and many brilliant scholars of West Bengal was then in full swing in West Bengal. The movement itself had a strong base in Presidency College and was led by Asim Chatterjee. While in erstwhile Bangladesh there was civil war. Both sides of Bengal were running through turbulent times. I expressed through Rakhal Sir, to my father, to allow me to take off for West Bengal and Calcutta for further studies. My father denied and thus I was admitted to Post Graduate Science and Art College, Raipur in the Faculty of Arts. It had an excellent campus.

Mr. Tandon, a Professor of Chemistry was our Principal. He looked like a pure Aryan and sometimes came to our hostel with the shrewd hostel warden Mr. N. H. Shukla. Mr. Tandon was receptive, gracious, dignified and frank. While he spoke, he smiled profusely. I was privileged to meet him, when he came to visit 'Shastri Hostel'. I stayed there with my friend Pratap Shankar. Mr. Tandon's personality during college hours on the campus was diametrically opposite. He was grave, seemed to be arrogant, imperious and exceedingly decisive. But he never could outplay my father in showmanship. During school hours my father expressed in every step, a sort of royalty like Alexander Selkirk in St. Juan Fernandes Island, "I am monarch of all I survey. My right there is none to dispute." To me, he was an emblem of the Ottoman Emperor. He was extremely proud of his extraordinary swaggering gait and trait till his death. Every morning when my sleep breaks, I wake and I feel like dying forlornly with the reminiscence of his bewildered death.

Chapter 3
Education Brings Enlightenment

1

To you Charlie my dear,

I am anonymously writing just as you did in your movement for the right destination. During my graduation, I was offered English Medium and English was my special subject. I had no tutor as I could not afford it. I wrote down notes in Hindi on my own and translated them to English. In the Faculty of Arts there were two very attractive ladies -- Mrs. Tasneem Engineer, wife of a multi-millionaire, a Parsee lady who was exuberantly beautiful, she was doing her B.A. final. Unfortunately, I had no chance to interact with her. My attire, half rural gait, scanty confidence, poor knowledge of Hindi and English, and above all my isolation without my mother did not let me live with my wits. The other was Miss Paramjit Kaur, a tall and fair girl whose father was a Sikh Brigadier. She came over to me and asked in Hindi, about the time table of English Literature class. I was jittered and overwhelmed. She did her schooling from a convent at Jalandhar and was fluent in English. I felt far inferior to her, yet started imagining that someday Paramjit would fall in love with me. She was the second lady whom I sincerely loved and dreamt to marry but was not brave enough to express my feelings. She belonged to a conservative family. Many powerful students of the college were after her, but she possessed a granite heart. I adored her and missed her. She was so graceful, dignified, reserved, receptive, ambitious and systematic. I was determined to surpass her in studies and outscored her in the M.A. examination. Our conversations overwhelmed me, although I managed to talk in Hindi. She had no romantic feelings though. Her father coincidentally got transferred to Calcutta almost at the same time when I arrived in the city. My local guardian was B.R. Das who was very strict and it was very difficult to satisfy him.

Meanwhile, the Indo- Pak war was running in full swing. Bhasha Andolan of Bangladesh had a remarkable momentum under the political leadership of Sheikh Mujibur Rahman, and refugees from Bangladesh kept pouring into West Bengal and Tripura to get rid of savagery and genocide of Khan Sena. Pakistani leaders then were Zulfikar Ali Bhutto and Yayha Khan. Ted Kennedy, the youngest brother of John Fitzgerald Kennedy, the late president of the USA came to Calcutta, visited the makeshift refugee camps. Indira Gandhi ran a global itinerary to the west and erstwhile U.S.S.R. to communicate the problems of the exodus of helpless masses from Bangladesh. She met Willy Brandt, the then Chancellor of erstwhile West Germany and Richard Milhouse Nixon, the US President. Mrs. Gandhi's visit to US was counted unimportant by President Nixon and his Secretary of State, Henry Kissinger. The Indo-Pak war broke out and General S.H.F.J. Manekshaw was the chief of the army staff.

Till 1964 January, my father stayed in erstwhile East Pakistan. Field Marshal Mohammed Ali Ayub Khan, a brilliant student of Sandhurst Military College of England was then the President of Pakistan. He was supremely able, ruthless, extremely handsome, non-communal, Machiavellian dictator. My father was an embodiment of monarch in the villages of East Pakistan. His classmate was Mr. Fazlul Kader Chowdhury, the then speaker of Pakistan. After the partition in 1947, East Pakistan was run by his friends who were Muslims. In undivided India while he was graduating from Barisal B.M. College, they adored him as a student. He was the hostel monitor. His friends wrote 'man eater' with a piece of chalk on his portal. He was not accustomed to the bureaucracy in democratic India. He worked in British India and then worked in Pakistan that was administered by Army officers.

We, the students in Shastri Hostel, keenly awaited every evening to listen to the last news bulletin on All India Radio. India was going ahead and Bangladesh was liberated by Indian Army under Jagjit Singh Arora. Mr. Niazi from Pakistan's end had to sign the paper of cognizance of defeat and surrender. I was overjoyed like others that ours was a strong nation and the strongest lady of the world was our Prime Minister Mrs Gandhi. Gradually the stupor of victory however dispelled.

While listening to such news I remember we as a family came from Bangladesh in 1964. I and my two elder brothers managed to get admitted to Mahesh Ramakrishna Mission School by kind consideration of the Swamiji, the headmaster Mihir Sir and Mr Bimal Nandy, a handsome and saintly teacher of the ashram. He was also from Batajore. My father managed to get him appointed hostel superintendent of ITI Hostel of Durgapur. The appointment letter reached him at 10am on 27th May, 1964. In the afternoon we came to know through A.I.R. the news of the sad demise of Pandit Jawaharlal Nehru. My father lost his job in five months' time. He was a strong disciplinarian and failed to be merely a hostel superintendent. He had been conditioned in all respect as a headmaster with grandiose personality in the rural parts of Barisal and Dhaka. He met Dr. Mohan Das who was the chairman of the Dandakaranya Refugee Project and the deputy Rehabilitation Minister of India. He was a very close relative in the in-law's family of my mother's third sister. Dr. Das was an embodiment of God to us and for many like us in DNK Project. My father joined Sukumar Sen Memorial High School at Umerkote, Koraput, and Orissa DMK as headmaster. His super dynamism worked like super dynamo. He earned high reputation as well as hostility. One morning, Mr. P. Pradhan, the zonal administrator happened to reach the school and called him. My father was then teaching the Selfish Giant by Oscar Wilde in Class IX. Through the messenger he requested him to wait. He got chagrined and left and complained to the chief administrator of the Project who summoned my father.

While he was acting headmaster of Khepupara High School of Barisal in the 40s, a British school inspector had come to visit and my father left the class to call on him. The inspector asked: "Mr. Sharma, where were you when I called?"

My father replied, "Sir, I was in my class." And the inspector said: "If Viscount Wavell comes to your school during school hours you must not leave your class before the bell goes." Since that day my father accepted this as holy diction from heaven.

Fortunately, Mr. S.C. Roy, the chief administrator of DNK Refugee Project was an ex-Captain in the British Army and understood why my father did not leave his class. He told: "Those were good old British days. Now you have to adjust with the officers on deputation in the biggest refugee project of the world, though no Prime Minister of India ever visited it."

My father got ultimately transferred to Kapsi High School, Bastar, Chattisgarh, within the periphery of DNK Project. It was a school in name only--- with a tin shade and bamboo walls and consisted of only five teachers along with my father, the headmaster. Again, he launched his odyssey with super dynamism, to improve the school with remarkably scanty means provided by DNK Project Administration. Each primary school from Class I to V was run by a single teacher and a headmaster! There was no ayah, no durwan. The total refugee project was in a take off stage and so was the school and my father as the commander.

It was during this time in 1965 that Indo-Pak War started. Lal Bahadur Shastri was the Prime Minister and my mother joined the Women Association to collect funds for the war by preparing and selling snacks in stalls they ran on our school ground during football tournaments and other functions. Kali Puja and Diwali were celebrated with grandeur at Kapsi, dramas were staged and I was given the role of Muazuddin, the youngest son of Tipu in a drama. I did not know why I was so delighted, and took a special fancy for the lady who played the role of Tipu Sultan's begum. I used to spend sleepless nights with romantic thoughts crossing my mind. I cried secretly when the drama was over. The night of the drama left an indelible spot in my mind.

2

Meanwhile, a massive school building was coming up at Pakhanjore, the capital of Paralkote Zone, 11kms from Kapsi. My father was trying to expedite the process and some of the bureaucrats were trying to start the school without him. The school was shifted with my father and other four teachers. In October 1967, I was in class VIII and my *mejda* was in Class IX. Dada was in Calcutta for higher studies. I did not like Pakhanjore in the beginning, but now I love to recall my life there.

Pakhanjore was a beautiful place. It had a transport office, a market place, a bus-stand, a big playground and then vast expanse of arid land beyond. The mountain ranges of Narayanpur was conspicuous in the distance. By the arid land, a road ran towards a dam site and on top there was a small hut with a tin shed and no walls. The Circuit House stood on a small hill. It looked more sophisticated. But I discovered that my romantic love for Kapsi was getting dispelled. My father became stricter with me, for I became more unintelligent in tackling the bohemian feelings that had been creeping in. Saraswati Puja of the school was always organized by my father. But I found myself unimportant even though I was sure that my potentials were not properly focused on. Though my father was always rude to me and always forced me to be ambitious, my mother filled in the gap as she had faith in me. My father was the first man in the whole world who would tell, "Sunder has an extraordinary brain, and if he works hard, he will make history." But my mother smiled with pride and said: "He is born with cow dung in his head." In spite of my father's high hopes, I did not fare well in the exams.

In the half-yearly examination, I secured sixty-six in English and four in Mathematics! I spoiled my time and energy whiling away at the boys' hostel. Though I got promoted to Class IX, all students of my class secured better marks than me. No girl of my class even looked at me, I was so inconspicuous. I had an infatuation for Chandrima, her father was Madhab Sen, a contractor, and during our stay at Kapsi, Chandrima's rich and beautiful mother once told my mother, "Sunder's face is exquisitely sweet and I will get my daughter married to him."

"Very good," returned my mother.

Chandrima was beautiful with slight mongoloid features. She was sent to Santiniketan for higher studies. She was excited when she heard what her mother said, but I did not express my delight. My dada asked me, "Hey! Do you feel proud?"

"Not at all," I replied. "What is it to me whether she stays in Santiniketan or in any other corner of the world." I replied hesitantly contorting my face as if her name was untouchable for me. In reality, I was obsessed with Chandrima. But my love for her gradually ceased to survive.

I had tremendous respect for Rakhal Sir, our Mathematics teacher. He was refined, bright eyed, lean and thin, clad in milky white ironed dhoti and kurta. I enjoyed sir's company. My parents had great affection for Sir. But once my father chatted inadvertently, "Sunder spoils his precious time following Rakhal babu." Sir happened to hear that. That evening he came back to his quarters from the volleyball ground, he caught hold of me and let me know that he knew about my father's comment. He forced me to reach his quarters every morning with books, copies and pen. Sir's efforts improved me academically, mentally and morally. Rakhal Sir enthused me, he was a staunch Subhashite and anti-Gandhian, so was I. Our school celebrated Gandhi centenary for a week with pomp and grandeur as well as Netaji Subhash Bose's birthday. I felt myself a prophet, a reformer, a pioneer, a great genius. My intelligence at that time did not let me measure my caliber and capacity. There was dangerous personality clash between my parents. The conflicts back home spoiled our growing up years to a great extent. Sometimes Rakhal Sir turned an intermediary to pacify my parents. I reached Class X. My *mejda* had gone through the School Final Examination securing 86% marks in Mathematics, the second highest marks in our area. There was a feeling of euphoria in our family. *Mejda* was sent to Calcutta for higher studies.

3

I remember that Wednesday vividly. It was raining torrentially when *Mejda* started on his journey. Me, my youngest brother and only sister were left with our parents. That evening, when a continuous downpour was hitting Bastar incessantly, my father embraced me, and said, "You will sit for the IAS examination and will be an officer and you will retire as a Governor." His words left no impression on me. I wanted to be an outstanding scholar with phenomenal academic performance. I neglected his ambition. Today, there is none to neglect and none to think that I could be a Governor. Definitely I wanted to be just a facsimile of Swami Vivekananda during the longest tenure of my adolescence. I was not immaculately concerned of my congenital demerits, diametrically opposite to the congenital merits of the great global monk. My ideas and opinion changed several times. Randomly I plunged into a sea of confusion. And still, I am not free from that adolescent deluge and always fail to anchor on to something. I pose myself and act before my colleagues and students as one of the greatest decisive personalities of the globe. I don't know whether they ridicule me.

A saint used to come to my father at Kapsi. Seeing me walking back from the school he once told my father, "This boy will be an outstanding great man of the world." I have been waiting till date to find the authenticity of the prediction. I ask myself, "Can I not be anything more than that?" I have been waiting to convey that message to the world which is yet to reach me.

I asked zero and the reply comes with a zero. This zero is nothing, this zero is everything. Adi Shankaracharya's 'Mayabad' and Nagarjuna's 'Sunyabad' divulged the unimportance of the world, the worldly life in the infinite universe. 'Sarva Khllidumm Brahma', this tenet was discovered and preached by Shankaracharya. But still, we are important. We are a part of the universe. Every individual is equal to the universe as the sun, the stars, and the galaxies. This voluminous decoration indicates that the universe knew that we were coming. The universal zero is the source of universal energy, strength and creation.

I ask myself, "Why should I give message to the world?"

The universe itself is ceaselessly expressing a supreme message in every aspect of creation, in every moment. It is preposterous to think myself the only individual, who reaches the world to convey the message from eternity. Each and every particle, from the largest to the tiniest is the messenger from the omnipotent, omniscient and omnipresent invisible power, and indomitable longing eternity.

Chapter 4
Fathoming Changes

1

My B.A. Preliminary Examination started in the first week of June in 1972. I boarded the down Bombay Mail via Nagpur from Raipur station in the evening, the very day I finished my examination. All other members of my family meanwhile reached Calcutta. I started for Calcutta alone. Next morning the down Bombay Mail reached Howrah station. After many years I met dada. During my stay in Orissa and erstwhile Madhya Pradesh for quite a long time, I literally forgot Bengal – its green fields, its people and the poor masses always suffering from ill health. I realized my enthusiasm to stay in Bengal had died gradually.

My father left for Pakhanjore alone as summer vacation of his school was over. My mother started a few days later with my sister and youngest brother. Khadu Bhai, my dada escorted them back to Pakhanjore. I stayed back violating my father's plan and it was then that I met Ranu di, eight years older to me. She was quite tall and slim with a dark complexion and had extremely romantic eyes. Her hair was curly and her voice was melodious, she was a great singer. In the first meeting, I was sort of hypnotized by her beauty. My dada and me would often go where she stayed for her nuptials, in downtown Calcutta. My love for her expressed roughly through respect, her affection for me was like an inundating river. It washed me away to a fathomless nothingness. I forgot my mother, my angry father, my sister and brothers. I forgot my mama bari, my didima – an embodiment of living goddess, my grandiose Ranga dadu. I forgot myself and began decking up as per Ranu di's choice.

Our love was unfathomable but was forced by our conscience to get it transformed into affection. A forced platonic love. Very likely there was no alternative for the remarkable difference of age and unparallel conservatism of our families. We both could not express our love as it was prohibited in our society. Secretly one can break the boundary of age. One can easily go voluptuous. But we did not do that. Her lilting mellifluous voice still rings in my memory, after almost three decades. In the evening, I used to walk with Ranu di by the Parnasree Lake and she told me once, "How will I spend my days without you Sonamoni?" I did not answer. It was not possible for me to reply. My throat got choked. I was a teenager then and head over heels in love with her. We walked around the lake silently. Some urchins chattered comments, taking us as genuine lovers. It was dusk and none could identify our age. She was beautifully dressed in a green silk sari and green blouse. Enigmatic smell of her perfume enchanted me. Much later, I managed to say, "How will I live without you Mamoni?" We called each other by these special names. We sat on the grass on the periphery of the government quarters.

"After going back to your college, will you write to me?" she asked.

"I will," I replied.

The environment of my college and that of Raipur was diametrically opposite to any college of Calcutta. She asked again, "Will you forget me?"

"I don't know," I replied somehow.

I had a flood of emotion but I was effortless to approach her with that emotion.

Meanwhile, I passed the B.A. preliminary and reached B.A finals. But the scheduled period fixed by Principal Mr. Tandon to get readmitted to Postgraduate Science and Arts College Raipur, was over. I had to join Durga College and lost all interest and ambitions. To my utter dismay, I discovered I had turned into a below average student. My father was able to fathom my downslide, but did not express his thoughts. I started paying more attention to my looks and to improve my accent in Hindi and English, rather than studies. My result in B.A. Final Examination was ridiculous, I myself was surprised. I just managed to pass through. The result was published on the evening of July 1974. My father was singing an Indian classical song on my mother's harmonium. I touched his feet and said, "Baba, I've become a graduate."

Hearing the percentage of marks he replied, "I'm awfully disappointed. I had high expectations from you." A few days after my results, my father sent me to Mr P N Mukherjee, the Superintendent of Education, DNK Project. Mr Mukherjee had been to England. His main office was at Kondagaon. He had put up at the circuit house. Back then, I had ultra-modern long hair and wore a costly yellow terricotton shirt that my dada gave as a Puja gift. My father sent me to him to speak about a job, if I could be appointed as a teacher of a primary school in Paralkote Zone. I met him and said: "Sir, I am the third son of Mr. N. C. Sharma. He sent me to talk to you to get myself employed as a teacher of a primary school."

He was a bit taken aback at my urbanized ultra-modern get up. He probably did not have confidence in me and thought I would not be able to struggle in any primary school of the project. Almost all the schools in DNK Project had maximum three teachers and five classes. He replied, "Tell your father that I advise you to continue your post-graduation in English from Raipur University." I went on to do my post-graduation and travelled from Bhilai to Raipur every day. I was staying at my cousin Ratna di's house. Ratna di was the eldest daughter of the second brother of my father. Her husband was working at the Bhilai Steel Plant. His son became wayward and was sent to my father for schooling. I proposed through my *mejda* that I would be staying at Bhilai and journey to Raipur for my M.A. classes daily. I only needed college fees and miscellaneous expenditure. My father agreed with a bit of reluctance.

"You may go, but never take up English, you will fare worse," he said. His forecast was absolutely flawless. My father did not want to spend money aimlessly. I was given Rs 25/ and managed a truck driver, Debi Singh to take me to Bhilai. Trucks used to go from our place to Raipur for various official purposes. The truck reached Bhanupratappur in the evening. It was near Narayanpur, a beautiful location. The DNK project administration had no rapport with the government of Madhya Pradesh and hence the truck driver Debi Singh did not wish to go any further. A tribal theatre of Chattisgarh was going to be staged that night and he wanted to enjoy it. I had no alternative but to get down.

2

I went to a house of a local Bengali for a free nocturnal meal, but after the meal I had to leave. I went in the dark as if the venue of my night halt was already fixed. I walked and walked and reached where the theatre was going on. The name of the drama was 'Chandeli Gonda' based on Indian revolution. The actors were talking in Chhattisgarhi dialect. I left without watching the entire drama and walked aimlessly in the dark when I met someone, who I shall never forget. He was a tribal, a middle aged chowkidar of a small wood working centre. He was sleeping with a lantern by his head. I approached him with confidence. The poor people in the world love to believe, love to trust. Hearing my condition, he allowed me to sleep on the floor on a flat piece of wood. He was sleeping at the door in a tattered bed and on the floor near the door I lay. I awoke early in the morning to catch hold of Debi Singh, the lorry driver. Meanwhile, he left for Raipur. Still, I did not feel nervous. I stood with my arms akimbo. Many truck drivers had night halt with their vehicles to enjoy 'Chandeli Gonda'. I met Tilakraj ji, who was in his early fifties.

I said: "Uncle ji, I am the son of the headmaster sahib of Pakhanjore. (Main moochwale guruji ka beta hoon) I'm the son of the master with long moustache."

He returned, "I will go late, but I'll arrange your take off in a lorry of another driver." (mein tera jaane ka bandobast kar doonga. Mujhe jaane me der hogi). He introduced me to Prasad ji, a lorry driver, also in his late fifties with grey hair and a short cropped white moustache. Again, I started with identical voice and identical language. It was dawn, Tilak uncle helped me. I was allowed to sit by Prasad ji in the lorry. He started at 7.00 am. I felt relaxed and slept. The lorry ran like an eagle. We reached Dalli Rajhara, famous for its iron ore deposits. It was under BSP (Bhilai Steel Plant) and later became the hotbed of Naxal Movement under Shankar Guha Neogi. Prasad uncle did not take any money from me but said, "Ao babu, main tumhe chai pilate hoon'(Come on boy, have a cup of tea with me)." I had it with snacks. He had friends in the truck. Prasadji paid. I did not dare to pay for his affectionate treatment, fearing that I may hurt his sentiments in the process. I reached Bhilai at noon. This experience made me feel again that Prasad uncle, Tilak Raj uncle are men that symbolize the true ethos of India.

I reached Ratna di's house and by evening Raipur on a train without ticket. I was used to it travelling ticketless! I met Subhash Majumder, my friend there who rented a room to study in his 'Post Graduate Science and Arts College' in BSc preliminary. He was a student from Pakhanjore. I borrowed Rs 90 from him and met the college registrar. He told in a rude voice to get the order written by the Head of the Department of the University in the Faculty of English. I managed to meet Dr N S Verma, expressed my problems briefly. He did not express minimum doubt, signed the form and did not ask me any question regarding paraphernalia papers, mark sheets etc. He encouraged me, though not with a flood of emotion. But I felt his affection. For him, I could do my MA in English.

I used to come from Bhilai every morning. My classes started by 7.30 am. On the very first morning, I was standing in the lawn of the Arts building, Miss Paramjit all of a sudden stood in front of me. I was dumbfounded. She was angelic in her green salwar suit. She said, "From where have you graduated?"

I replied, "From Durga Arts College."

Then she asked, "Where do you stay here?"

I answered, "I come from Bhilai."

She was surprised. We sat in the first class of post-graduation with another student from Rajnandgaon. Dr NS Verma started with the history of English Literature. He talked, discussed in fluent English. In 1971 the entire scenario was otherwise. Miss Kaur was always reserved, conservative, mature and original. I hold her in high esteem.

"How do you like Bernard Shaw's St. Joan?" she asked me one day.

I replied, "I don't enjoy it. It seems too dull."

In fact, I did not even try to read the book, but lied to her. Once in class, in the absence of our teacher we discussed about our future career plans. She said, "I would like to appear for the IAS Examination after my post-graduation. And you should also try to do the same. You have already become far more powerful than what you used to be three years ago."

I replied, "I can't take a risk. My father is on the verge of retirement."

Once we both tried to bunk a class. Other classmates were absent. At Raipur, very few students did post-graduation in English. First, I went outside the building, and she brought my books from the class, though casually but I felt that she did it meticulously. I have often succumbed to this kind of emotional turmoil ever and anon, and was befooled. Now very likely I have learnt not to be befooled any longer. Kaur secured the highest marks in BA Finals from college. While I only, and don't know why I had the illusion of building an excellent career in spite of my inborn academic mediocrity. In Ravishankar University, students could do post-graduation from college. So, I joined the college from where I did my graduation for doing my masters.

3

I was sandwiched with day-to-day problems. I never lost hope to fulfill the target. And it was neither fixed nor known to me. I realize it today. I stayed at Bhilai, Sector 7, Street 20 in the quarters of my cousin. I usually woke up around 5.30am. There was no separate bed for any of us. I didn't even have time for ablution, just put on my trousers, shirt and a black full sleeved sweater during winter, ran amuck to the Bhilainagar Railway Station to board the train at 6am without a ticket. After getting down at Raipur railway station, I had no money to reach my college. I walked down railway lines, ran behind the engineering college. On the right-hand side was the Birdi Colony where my friend Subhash Majumder lived. Sometimes I ran like a mad street dog to attend the first class and mostly was able to do it. Without my illusory dream this kennel run would have become impossible. But Miss Kaur was never actually my cup of tea. When the class was over, I reached the station again in a similar way. My pangs were indescribable. It is still indescribable, only dimension is entirely different. I never thought Paramjit was my only solace and respite. It was my fault and my infirmity, which did not let me think during stress and strain about her, I asked myself, "Will I be able to surpass them all in all respects?" I got a reply from within, "Yes. I will be able to."

In the morning, when I started, I had no chance to pack a tiffin. In such times, Subhash Majumder came to my rescue, he was so kind. One evening I was returning from Raipur to Bhilai, at Kumhari Station a ticket checker entered the train. I jumped out of the compartment through another door and there was no other train. I walked, walked and walked. I reached Ratna di's quarters almost at 2am. Oh God! I don't know how I could do that!

In December 1974, my father came to Bhilai for his ear treatment. I went to Durg to receive him. There was no bus service directly from Pakhanjore to Bhilai. From Durg my father climbed a tempo and I was following it on a bicycle. My father reached much earlier.

He said, "You are a funny boy, you have no practical idea, how your old father would reach with minimum comfort."

He was walking with a big suitcase. At Bhilai, as I was not under my father's diktats and he was free from tension, I discovered a new amicable and an affectionate father. His expression became identical with that of my mother. "Do you smoke?" he asked me.

"No, not at all," I replied.

"Don't forget that I am a teetotaler and possess a very strong character," he added.

But the truth was I smoked quite often, and drank rarely. One fine morning he said, "Let us go for a walk." I followed him.

"Why don't you take care of your health? You are following your mother's path and will die early," said my father.

I smiled and walked with him from Sector 7. We reached Sector 9, and through the main road of Bhilai we reached Sector 5. The sun rose. "Let's go back my Sunny."

In his rare excellent mood, he addressed me 'Sunny'. Once during his stay at Bhilai, I fell sick. After coming back from my class, I did not take any meal and drank a glass of water with lemon. He knew it. "I depend on you and you are the only hope of mine, if your health fails this way, I am afraid, my hope will be unfulfilled," my apparently stubborn and obstinate father reacted when he felt that I had been neglecting my health. Today I am alone, alone in the desert of mankind. My parents are no more to ask about my well-being.

My mother went to Calcutta to meet Sunder mama, my second maternal uncle. He came from England in December'74. Ma wrote she would return to Pakhanjore through Bhilai. Early morning, me and father went to Bhilainagar Station to receive her as she was travelling on Bombay Mail via Nagpur. We spent a few days together till they left and I went to Durg bus-stand to see them off. I wept openly as I realized I shall never be with my parents again, enjoy the security they provided, the privileged and happy life they gave me.

As their bus whisked off, I stood there alone, tears streaming down. Somehow, I gathered myself and bicycled back to Bhilai. My *jijaji* was waiting for my return and somehow his affection, frankness and pride for me always enthused me. He used to say: "My brother-in-law is a brilliant boy." Back then, I never counted his words as important, rather I thought he was an insignificant, unimportant and ordinary looking man. My illusion did not make me realise and identify who my real friends in life were and who all to trust. Today I realize if my brother-in-law Gopal Chakraborty was not there in my life, I would not have been able to do my graduation and post-graduation. Many good people are born in this world to help others and most of them die as unsung heroes. On my train journeys along the JD Train (Jharsuguda Dongargarh) from Raipur, I met Jaharda, a senior Bengali man from Bhilai, who worked in the LIC. He would say: "In the entire JD you are the smartest one, and you are a Bengali, we feel proud of you." Such remarks spoiled me to some extent and I became conceited. I did not try at all to discover the true human potential in me. I had been journeying to prove myself. Consequently, my voyage is still on. I still do not have the right or power to tell my students, "Let the dead bury the dead, follow thou me."

In March 1975, I went home to prepare for my MA Previous Examination. My father shifted to another quarter, though much small, but it had electricity. Pakhanjore was gradually becoming a so-called modern town, losing its mystic beauty. I began disliking it. My father stopped talking to me like he did before. I was missing that father, whom I met at Bhilai a few months ago. After my return, I found he had not changed much. When I was a student of Class VIII, he used to teach me. One day while teaching William Blake's 'Songs of Innocence' and 'Songs of Experience', he retorted, "Your professors do not know English. You should have done your MA as a private candidate under my guidance."

I dared not reply. He had graduated from Barisal BM College and famous Bengali poet Jibanananda Das was one of his teachers. My dad was the hostel monitor in BM College, while Professor Moni Kanta Ganguly, 1st Class 1st gold medalist in English from Calcutta University was his hostel superintendent. Dad used to say: "My Sir was extremely disciplined. He rose early in the morning at 4am and went to bed by 10.30pm." I heard from him that later Ganguly became vice-chancellor of Shillong University.

Father taught me classics like 'Tess D'Urbervilles' by Thomas Hardy. He was a great fan of Hardy. "Do you know that Hardy wrote about our life? That human life is always led by an invisible force, so nothing can be decided by us." He used to quote the exact words of Thomas Hardy. He also spoke of Jibanananda Das.

"We never saw JD attend any meeting, symposium, gathering, funeral or condolence meeting. We didn't know that Sir would be so great in future. We did not try to fathom him owing to his aloofness as he spent hours with nature. Once in our class Prof. Das asked whether we had read 'Anna Karenina' of Lev Tolstoy. I replied that I had and he asked me to stand up and got to know that I had just seen the movie. Sir burst out laughing as he understood I did not read the book, but saw the movie and hence when questioned about the famous story, I could reply well. It was a rare opportunity for me to see Jibanananda Das burst out laughing in the class, that too with so much uproar. He had a habit of bringing out his tongue after finishing a part of a sentence."

Surprisingly, my father was not that proud of being a student of poet Jibanananda Das, rather he was proud of Prof Moni Kanta Ganguly and his Principal, Prof, Sailen Ghosh. Prof Ghosh had been to Harvard University for 22 years. He fled India and reached United States and his friends Manabendra Roy and Rashbehari Bose reached USSR (formerly) and Japan respectively. They did not surrender to the British Government in India. But Prof Ghosh, a physicist, married an American lady and gave a declaration to the British Government that he would in no way be involved with any kind of anti-British work in India. I heard from dad that he had the most dazzling face, was of short height and always wore khadi. He was simple but had a striking personality.

"Father, did he know you?" I had once asked. "Yes, I was not good in studies but I was well known to all as the most courageous and strongest boy," answered my father. "On one occasion I went to invite my principal along with his family for a night feast in our hostel. Sir immediately agreed and so did his spouse and daughters. I hired a horse drawn cart (it was the only means of transport in the town at that time), but Mrs Ghosh told me to sit by her and made their younger daughter sit on her lap. Thus, we reached our hostel along with our guest-in-chief."

4

Meanwhile, my studies got hampered a lot due to a student agitation at Pakhanjore High School over a got-up food grain crisis. It was done by some businessmen of Pakhanjore market in connivance with the local police station. The movement started with my father's support, but for some local surreptitious political mal practitioners it ultimately went against him. During this chaos, a girl went against the school rules and was suspended by my father. I subsequently went to the market of Pakhanjore and found a big poster against my father: 'Who is the Hero of Girls' Torture—Headmaster Sharma!'

Passersby thronged to look at it and I lost my temper with some ex-students of the school. Dhiraj, an ex-student of my father got down from his bicycle to beat me up but I was saved by Mr Ramesh Srivastava, husband of Hindi teacher Sashiprabha Srivastava. He told them, "Whom are you going to beat in the open market place? His father Mr N C Sharma was your headmaster. Will you beat him up and express your gratitude!" There were 3 of them -- Dhiraj Mistry, the first boy in my *mejda*'s class, Prantosh Hira, the second who was first boy of class VIII when I was a student of Class VI, the third was Ananda Bepari, junior to me by one year. Fortunately, Uncle Srivastava was there to save me, else I would have been badly beaten up by the erstwhile sycophants. In fact, my father nurtured sycophancy and adulation sometimes.

Dhiraj shouted: "I allow you to go bastard. We can even kill your father." I was trembling in anger and fear. Just three and a half years ago, this very Dhiraj had presented my father a costly shawl. Later in 1975 July, Prantosh wrote to him and Ananda apologized. My father did not react to any of these incidents. I came back home and tried to pay attention to my studies. My mother could read my face and said, "What happened, you look upset."

"Nothing!" I told.

After dinner, my mother used to prepare a cup tea for me so that I could study into the late hours. During my stay at

Pakhanjore, all pseudo revolutionaries came and apologized to my father. Even today, I have many pseudo friends and many foes like 'paper tigers.' My mother had firm faith in me and my father had high hopes for me. I felt that my mother was proud of my father and so was my father's feelings towards my mother. But they never expressed it. Our interaction with our outstandingly affectionate mother was so acute that I can always recollect her innumerable conversations and every sentence of my father is my reminiscence. He spoke to me like an oracle.

Meanwhile, my examination neared. I readied for Raipur. One evening my father ordered me to sit by him. I sat. "I am unable to run the expenditure of your studies. Mukti (my only sister) will pass the HS this year. Dipu (my youngest brother) will do the same two years later. You must seek a job. You go and meet Mr Sunil Halder, the deputy chief township engineer of Bhilai Steel Plant. He is the brother-in-law of my brother-in-law and an issueless person. Go, and request him to get you employed," he said. It was dusk, a summertime evening at Bastar. My mother had gone somewhere. I felt dejected and dull. Mr Sunil Halder was well known to me. He was the eldest brother of my *bara mamima.* He had six brothers and he helped none. There was no chance that he would help me. Anyway, before my departure for Raipur and before bidding farewell to the pseudo revolution of the students of Pakhanjore Higher Secondary School, some hooligans from Kanker College were called by those revolutionaries and their notorious senior guides along with an MLA to teach my father a good lesson. It was a dry warm afternoon and some boys of the school came from the 'tent' where the office of the agitators was installed. It was near the main road of Pakhanjore, between the HS school boundary and the primary school.

"Sir, an MLA has come along with some volunteers to meet you," the students told my father.

My father could not make head or tail of it. He was reading 'Science Today,' an article on scientist Satyendra Nath Bose, published after the demise of Prof Bose. He said: "You take *guruji*, Mr RD Prasad our teacher."

"No Sir, they only want to meet you," they replied.

My father changed his dress from l*ungi* to *dhoti* and put on an ordinary full-sleeve shirt, and reached the venue walking through the tremendous heat. Apprehending something was wrong, I reached too with my youngest brother. Eight hooligans from Kanker College cordoned him off; the MLA was sitting in one corner like an embryo. One of the fat *goondas* said to my father in Hindi, "Did you punish the girl?"

My father replied in English, "Who the hell are you to ask me question like this! She is my daughter and it is entirely my look out."

They forced my father to speak in Hindi and my father shouted at him. "Shut up!"

All eight hooligans stood up, but my father angrily said, "Come on, come on my children. I am an ex-military man." My brother and me got agitated and did not know what to do. But the beastlike nincompoops did not dare come forward to my father.

Seeing me outside the tent, dad chased me: "Why did you come to save me? Am I not sufficient to thrash these scoundrels!" my father growled like an old wounded tiger. We returned home, Ma was accustomed to this kind of situation for my father had been facing hassles and chaos almost always in his service life. Moreover, the DNK project administration was being run by hordes of incompetent bureaucrats. It was generally gliding to collapse.

"What were they doing?" asked my mother.

"They organized hooligans to threaten father and his counter attack was dynamic," I told her.

"Your father shook off many corrupt school committees during his stay in East Pakistan (Bangladesh)," she returned with pride.

On the onset of my journey to Raipur, I was reminded by my father to look for a job. I decided not to return to my parents again. Foolishly, I hurled myself into the topsy turvy world.

Chapter 5
Making of a Young Man

1

I reached Raipur, not fully prepared for the MA exam. Before my departure from Pakhanjore, I dropped a postcard to Dr N S Verma, the Head of the Department of English of our University. I did not expect reply but he replied. Reaching Raipur, I went to Sir's quarters. "Sharma, I had your postcard. You are not to worry. Things are entirely up to God," he said. And I became enthusiastic once again. But every time I left home and reached Raipur I used to be in a stupor, for my mother.

"I know a face, a lovely face,
As full of beauty as of Grace;
The face itself like a joy
To have seen it I am a lucky boy.
I have seen that have few other,
This lovely woman is my mother."

I sometimes thought of what would happen to me after my mother's death, the very thought bewildered me. But look at me, my mother died and I am still living, I had neglected her, gave her money but no comfort. I imagined she would live long. Whenever I am deeply depressed, a face floats before my eyes, that of Sri Ramakrishna Paramhansa and the temple of Dakshineshwar.

Anyway, I appeared for the MA Previous Examination in 1975. On the first day I was unable to locate my seat. A vexed Miss Kaur pointed to my chair. I was overwhelmed by her help and wrote the examination. I used to come from Birdi Colony where I had put up in a hired house. It was behind the engineering college of Raipur across the railway line. I had to reach my friend's hired house leaving the Raipur stadium on the left. I had missed many chapters, like I did not read 'St Joan' of GBS, 'Cocktail Party' of TS Elliot, 'Eve of St Agnes' of John Keats. I started studying late into the night, bought packets of Charminar cigarettes, smoked to get rid of drowsiness. My father was a total abstainer. He found no difference between a murderer and a smoker. For his third son it would become far more internecine.

I somehow managed to finish the examination. I owe Subhash for this, as well as to Ratna di of Bhilai. Without them, I would have not done my MA in English. Meanwhile, I dashed a letter to my dada (eldest brother) in Calcutta stating the problem I was facing to continue with my studies. He replied, "Don't worry, for a boy with a charming personality like you, there will be no problem in getting you employed in any stop-gap job in Calcutta. You will be able to continue your studies for the MA Final."

I availed students' railway concession and boarded the down Bombay Mail in the evening from Raipur Railway Station with Rs 5/ in my pocket. Uncle Ramesh Srivastava and Ashoke Sen, a student of BA Final from Pakhanjore sent me off. Ashoke borrowed Rs 5/ from me many months ago and on the evening of my departure he could not manage to pay back. He asked Srivastava uncle at the station, "Uncleji would you be kind enough to lend me Rs 5/? I will pay you back later." Srivastava ji paid him then and there. He told me, "(Jaldi laut aana) Come back as early as possible. If you pass the MA Previous you have to resume your studies again."

The train whistled and started to move. Uncle Srivastava and Ashoke stood on the platform, waving and I left Raipur to seek home in Calcutta. Uncle's arrival on that day was a sheer coincidence. Later I met him only once in 1976, after appearing for my MA Final examination. And in 1998, a few months after my mother's death, my father handed me an invitation card of uncle's funeral rites!

I reached Howrah next morning, I had not informed my *mejda* about my arrival. My elder brother reached the station but failed to locate me. I got extremely nervous. I had never travelled to Calcutta without any companion before. So, I asked a dhoti clad gentleman: "*Dada* can you tell me how to reach the bus stop to avail a 12C bus for Behala?" He told me the directions. I had only one luggage with me. I left all my books and miscellaneous belongings with Subhash. I managed to reach 567 DH Road, the only respite where my *dada* came for adda. I found him seated and he asked his friend, "Dilip, did you get any telegram, Sunder was supposed to reach Calcutta."

"No, I received nothing," he replied. My *dada* jumped when he saw me. It was beyond his expectation, for he came back being disappointed from Howrah station. After reaching Calcutta, my sufferings increased. Listening to my problems my *dada* applied on my behalf seeing an advertisement in the newspaper for the job of a counter salesman in a showroom opposite Triangular Park on Rash Behari Avenue. My brother escorted me to the venue of the interview. It was raining and we had a single umbrella. My loving eldest brother got completely drenched to protect me. I lost my temper and shouted at him, "Why are you harassing me in this way? I will not face the interview." He knew me, remained silent, as my mother did when I lost my temper. I faced the interview and got the job.

When I started from our place in Behala to the shop, there was no bus and a heavy downpour was on. *Dada* had high fever, yet he said: "Kalubhai, you are not to worry, I shall give you a lift on my bicycle." It was Monday. On RB Avenue all shops open at 3pm on Mondays. My hardworking affectionate dada had me seated on the rod of the bicycle, it was raining torrentially and he was cycling with all his might and we reached the shop on time. In my boyhood I had a sun burnt complexion, so I was addressed as Kalubhai, Kalu Mian or Kali by dada. I was amazed with the charm and grandeur of RB Avenue. There were two more sales girls, though they were elder to me, we became good friends. There was one middle-aged manager, he liked me but I failed to realize it.

"Come back to Raipur and resume your studies," ordered my father in a postcard one day. "I am prepared to go to any part of the world to build up my life," I returned desperately. One fine evening while I was doing my duty in the showroom very religiously, my dada and mejda arrived and called me outside. No relative of any employee in the showroom was allowed to come inside during busy schedule. Both of them embraced me. "You have done very well in your MA previous Examination. You have secured more than 53.3% marks," told my mejda with ecstasy. That was the last comparatively good result in my life. I never secured good marks again, though I continued my MA Final as a private candidate.

2

India at that time was running through Emergency Period. Indira Gandhi declared 'Emergency' on June 26, 1975. The disheveled country had a better look. MISA (Maintenance of Internal Security Act) was imposed on various matters. Trains were reaching and leaving right on time. Ticket checkers for long journey forgot to demand extra money for allocation of seats. People in Sales Tax, Income Tax and Customs put their feet in the shoes of ticket checkers. My MA Finals was scheduled to be held on 5th April, 1976. Had there been no emergency, the scheduled date of the examination would have been postponed as it used to be before. But Emergency created external discipline and internal cancer in democratic India. I ransacked College Street but could not collect all the books I needed. I was constrained to go to Raipur to fill in the form for my MA Finals. I met Mr Ranganna, the then Head of the Department of English. I entreated him to allow me to appear for my examination as a regular candidate. "If you can leave your job and attend classes regularly, I will allow you," he replied.

So, I reached our Pakhanjore quarters with a small luggage. My father was alone reading a newspaper with a lantern on the table. In those days we had frequent power cuts. My father saw me and shuddered, "Where is Dipu?" he asked. My youngest brother had also gone to Calcutta for medical treatment. "He is all right in Calcutta and improving gradually," I returned. My mother had gone to the house of our neighbor to attend '*Ramnaam Kirtan*'. It was a regular Saturday ritual. I went to meet my mother and sister. At first Ma could not recognize me as I had a shawl on my head. But then she jumped in joy, "I mistook you for a girl," she smiled. It was heavenly. No smile in the whole world is sweeter to me than her smile. It expressed her affection, love, blessing, excuse, pleasure, ecstasy and every positive aspect of the world.

I stayed at Pakhanjore for three days, some of the best days of my life. We sang, gossiped, cried, walked through the undulating fields. My *mejda* was my best companion all through. My father came home one afternoon at school break and asked: "Do you want to stay or go back?"

"I don't want to go back to Calcutta again," I replied.

"Naukri chhor do (Leave your job in Calcutta immediately)," returned my jolly father with a smile. I could not leave my job. I left my father, mother, *mejda*, and my little sister instead. I left Pakhanjore. And I reached Raipur again, filled the form and went to the court to get it signed by a first-class magistrate with my friend Ashoke. I joined my hands and folded to convey my *namaskar* (regards) obsequiously to the magistrate who was a true gentleman. The previous night the Principal of the Chattisgarh College signed my form as token of recognition. He did not know me, did not see me before, even then he signed. I did not know the name of that deified personality, but he gave a recognition which is unforgettable and Ashoke was with me. While Indira Gandhiji's Emergency was on, India turned into a police state. Yet people like N S Verma, Mr Ranganna and the principal of Chattisgarh College were all good men who were part of my blessed world.

I left the form and money with Ashoke, had a bath in a big pond near Birdhi Colony, washed my shirt and got it dried, had my trunk from Subhash, reached Durg, and availed down Bombay Mail with Ashoke. Ashoke got down at Raipur. He helped me all through the final year of my post- graduation. I met the ticket checker. He was Mr Goswamy. I wanted to avail a seat. I was allotted the same and without any extra charge. None dared charge extra money as Emergency was in action. I came back to Calcutta again. It is the city of my failure, the city of my success, it is the city of my frustration, of my enthusiasm, of hatred hurled upon me, of love poured on me, the city of my dreams, my savior, my love, the city where I am loved. It is also the city where I cremated my mother – my goddess and it is the city where I cremated my father – my headmaster, my mentor, my teacher, my friend, my philosopher, my guide.

Anyway, I got down at the platform with the trunk on my shoulder and reached the queue of the store room to keep the heavy trunk on the luggage rack. I was unshaven since I left Calcutta. I had a dirty shirt on and tied the second-hand sweater around my neck. "Are you a driver?" asked a tall North Indian gentleman. "No, I am a salesman in a departmental store," I replied with pride. I had a false reverie that once I would be one of the most important men of all time. My turn came, I kept the trunk on the rack and had the receipt after a meager payment. I requested the caretaker to look after it, "Sir, please pay attention to my poor luggage," said I. "Oh! Definitely, with utmost care. Please spare a few *annas* so that I can have snacks and tea." I gave him, he took it without any hesitation.

Innumerable series of incidents were awaiting me. I straightaway went to the departmental store to join my duty, but was told by the proprietor not to join but to go back home. Mr Prabir Sircar, the proprietor, was an excellent man otherwise. I have high regards for him and his spouse Mrs Lipika Sircar. They never displayed their affection exuberantly for me, but I felt it. In the far bigger periphery of my life, I miss them, I miss their love, their uncontroversial faith in me. Mrs Sircar had honours in English and Mr Sircar was a commerce graduate. He was tall, fair complexioned, bespectacled gentleman of forty-three. Mrs Sircar was tall, a bit dark, cultured and extremely simple at heart, highly sophisticated, modern and stylish.

When I joined the departmental store, it was like heaven to me. I met many celebrities of Calcutta during my stay as a salesman on the counter. One of them was Shakuntala Devi, the prodigy of Mathematics. Me and my father were remarkably weak in mathematics. I told Shakuntala Devi, "Madam, I am remarkably weak in mathematics." "No problem, many great men of the world are weak in mathematics," she had replied. She showed me her photograph with Yehudi Menuhin, Ava Gardner and Indira Gandhi. She invited me to attend an exhibition that she was preparing in a hotel of Calcutta. "Do come, you will enjoy it," she told. "Yes ma'm, definitely I will," I returned. I knew I would never go. The only program I enjoyed during that period was a whole night 'Indian Classical Music Programme' during the winter of 1975 in 'Banga Sanskriti Sammelan.' I liked the song of Bhismadev Chattopadhyay *"Jadi mane pare sedinero—o katha, amare bhulio priye"* (Oh my love, if the reminiscence of that day arrives, you forget me, and you forget me.) His voice resembled that of my father. The musical function got over in the wee hours of the morning. I was astounded to see the quality of people in the audience. They were all so cultured and dignified.

I tried to resume my studies but could not cope with the duty and studies. It was extremely difficult to collect books from the bookstalls of College Street frequently. Once my *dada* told, "Today I will accompany you." "Ok, I will be privileged," I replied. We both went to College Street and I began to search for my coveted books. "Oh! It's really a difficult task," retorted my dada after hopping between stalls. Seeing his contorted face, I managed somehow to buy some of the books and ran in a double decker bus towards my working spot.

3

During my service as a counter salesman, I saw innumerable beautiful couples, ladies, gentlemen, and hordes of super attractive young girls. I in fact was not accustomed to it. My past life did not allow me any chance likewise. It seemed that every young girl was 'la belle dame sans merci'. I was really passing through an outstandingly attractive and boring period of my life. I felt acute disorder in my digestive system. I did not have a single friend in Calcutta. I was craving for a friend, preferably a girlfriend. "Am I so unattractive that not a single girl comes to me with love and inspiration!" I asked my *dada.*

"Why will they come to you? You have to approach them," he returned. "I dare not and I think that I am not that important," I said to him.

"Then sit idle and meditate for Urvashi," he replied.

Indira Gandhi's Emergency was on and the date of my MA Final. Though I readied myself with luggage I was almost unprepared to sit for any easy test in the world. Probably I boarded the up Bombay Mail, reached Raipur, had my admit card but found no room for my stay during the tenure of my examination. I went to Subhash Majumder, my friend in Birdhi Colony. "Can I stay with you?" I asked.

"It's very difficult this time, you have to go to Durga Arts College every morning from here. It will be too expensive. Apart from that my room partner will not agree," he replied.

I went to my friends of Pakhanjore at Hotel Kallol (Raipur Lodge). Every ex-student of my father politely and dexterously gave a negative reply. I met Kamal Kishore Sharma, my MA Previous batch mate from Rajnand Gaon. He gave me shelter in his room in the hostel of Durga College. "Don't you worry, I am there for you. Don't get so upset. Let's go and have tea from a nearby stall." His kindness was beyond imagination.

I appeared for my MA Final almost without any preparation. At the time of my departure from Calcutta for my examination, my *dada* and *chotomama* came to see me off. My *dada* loved me beyond measure. He gave me a self-addressed post card, so that despite my busy schedule I might manage to write a letter to him. "Don't forget to write to me every three days. I cannot live without you," he repeatedly told me. "Yes, I will," I returned casually. At that time, I would always fail to understand his deep love for me. Reaching Raipur, I did not write a single letter to him. Even the self-addressed post card that I was given remained in my bag like a token of negligence. I was offered Linguistic as a special paper and did not read a single book.

"Kamal will you help me after supper?" I asked Kamal Kishore. Till 2am he went on helping me with my studies.

"Yaar I am getting tired. Please allow me to sleep," he went off to sleep. I was the only student in the Durga College hostel who went on smoking cigarettes and pouring through the books aimlessly to get prepared for the next morning's exam. I finished three packets of cigarettes in a single night!

I finished my written papers somehow. My viva voce was next, the external examiner was very likely coming from Nagpur University. I got myself properly shaven, wore my blue shirt and best pair of trousers. Mr Ranganna, the Head of the Department of English was sitting with the middle-aged External Examiner. They were both extremely nice to me. Usually before any battle starts, I get nervous, but on the battlefield any sort of tension and nervousness just evaporates.

I entered the room for viva voce. "Which paper in your MA Final was the most satisfactory?" asked the external examiner.

"American Literature Sir," I replied. Both the professors went on asking me all possible easy questions from American Literature. I fumbled with my answers, I did not know them. But I came out as a hero. Miss Paramjit, Kamal Kishore, one South Indian lady (she was a candidate) were waiting outside in the verandah to know about the skirmishes going on inside. The south Indian lady asked, "What did they ask you? How did you reply? What was their action and reaction?"

While I was talking to her, I was talking with a British accent. "You speak in a British accent," commented the lady.

"Do you know Ma'm in '71 he didn't even know how to speak in English. He has improved a lot," told Miss Paramjit.

She had my address. I had only one similarity with her. I came to Calcutta in 1975 from Raipur and her father (a brigadier) got transferred to Calcutta in 1975. "I will meet you in Calcutta. I hear that you are working under a jeweler, I will buy a diamond." That was her last dialogue and that was our last meeting. Still, I hold her in esteem and affection.

I started for Bhilai the next day and borrowed Rs 10/ from Kamal Kishore. And I have not yet paid him back. My father had put up in Ratna di's house, for my sister was appearing for the BA Preliminary Examination as a private candidate. I reached them with my friend Ashoke Sen. "Sunder, Ratna is angry with you. Go and give her a hug. She is your didi," told my father. I ran to Ratnadi. She was screaming. I lifted her in my arms and brought her to my father. "Ha ha ha ha, at last you are successful to do both the tough works together. You have lifted your *didi* and you melted her avalanche of anger," told my father in joy.

I stayed at Bhilai for two nights and started for Pakhanjore. "Don't leave for Calcutta from Pakhanjore till I come back," my father warned when I touched his feet. I stayed with my mother, my *mejda* till then.

After reaching Calcutta I went to join that departmental store and found a skinny stupid looking man senior to me by at least five years working in my place. I ran to Prabir da. My *dada* was with me. Mr Sircar expressed his inability to allow me to join again. I became terribly dejected. Prabir da had a one-eyed sycophant who used to misguide him most of the time. I was offered a job in Lisco Enterprise. My work was to sell sanitary napkins called Nature on purely commission basis. "Prabir da how will I survive in this dark world without your help," I asked. "Don't you worry, accept the challenge and go forward," he answered "Come tomorrow morning to the office of Lisco Enterprise and meet the manager." I was given the address. Next morning, I reached on time and I was given instruction by Prabir Sircar how to go about my new job.

Chapter 6
Joining as a Teacher

1

Dear Charlie,

I lost my world, my glamour and plunged into the life of a peddlar. My work was to collect order from the chemists' shop and houses, the suppliers had the responsibility to give things as per the orders collected. I was given a sample too. I trudged along the streets of Calcutta from Tala to Tollygunge during the summer of '76 selling the sanitary napkins. I somehow managed to collect large number of orders, but the supplier did not supply on time. He was a middle-aged man and looked like a pirate and resembled some of our political dadas. "Prabirda, Anup does not supply sanitary napkins to the chemist shops and houses in accordance with my order," I complained to the owner.

"Ok ask him to meet me. I will instruct him to help you out," said Prabir da.

A commotion inside Lisco Enterprise started after my complaint. Deliberate non-cooperation took a worse shape. Anup's supporters were the administrators of that small organization. Mr Sircar was helpless. I was losing enthusiasm, energy and physical strength due to this constant friction at the workplace. My health was worsening and I thought of returning to my parents. Nonetheless I was very ambitious.

I went to the American Consulate and met Mr Bacchu Roy to know how one can go to the United States, though he was not of much help. I began dreaming about my life and career, standing on a zero platform, but that proved to be one of my starting points. Our family too was facing problems at Pakhanjore. My most hard working, most responsible and brilliant *mejda* suddenly married, though he was still not employed. My father was flustered. The result of my MA Examination was announced and I managed to get through somehow.

"Come back to Pakhanjore immediately," wrote my mother. She always dreamt to get us settled down in Calcutta. But her dream died. My dada told me, "This evening we shall go to New Market and to some shops in Esplanade, so that you may get at least a job of a counter sales man." I went with him, but was rejected by all. I was tired and so was my Dada. My voice choked out of the insult and humiliation that we both had to undergo. "No leave it, let us go to Outram Ghat and relax," said my dada. It was dusk. Both dada and I sat and had ice creams. I shared with him how Lisco Enterprise was deliberately killing my congenital enterprise. I did not meet Prabir da because he was too good a man to judge the notoriety of the sycophants hanging around him. "Kali, let us go back home," said my dada while I was in a stupor, sitting at the Outram Ghat.

Struggle! Struggle! Struggle! Oh! Really, we all get tired. But as the struggle intensified, I became more ambitious, imaginative, desperate and promising. "The Calcuttans think that there is no university in the world equal to that of Calcutta and I am an ordinary post graduate from Raipur University. I should go back to Pakhanjore," I told my dada. He was anxious too. A post card came from my mother. She wrote, "Shakti, got married on 11th June 1976 at the Kalibari of Raipur. Your father has accepted the marriage." My father was on the verge of retirement. My dada had a small job. I was a peddler. My sister was yet to be married.

One fine morning I opened the bag where I kept the samples of Lisco Enterprise. I asked my dada, "Should I throw it away?"

"Yes, immediately," he replied. I threw away the samples immediately.

My poverty crossed all limits. Repair and renewal work of the palatial building of my Ranga dadu was going under the supervision of my baro mama. He needed a caretaker who would demand no charge probably. "Will you spare Sunder to do the work?" asked my baro mama to dada. "Yes, I can. He is now quite at a loss," replied my dada.

I reached Uttarpara and began working with full enthusiasm. It was a big building with an L shaped lawn. A preparation was going on to celebrate the marriage ceremony of Kutti. And it was a voluminous task. The final decision of that house was in general sent from England by my Sunder mama. My Ranga dadu was the direct disciple of Sarada Ma and my didi ma, disciple of Swami Akhandananda (Gangadhar Maharaj). Swami Akhandananda was one of the apostles of Sri Ramakrishna. Swami Vivekananda called him "Ganges". They were bosom friends and met Swami Vivekananda time and again when both were travelling India as *Paribrajaka.*

Swami Akhandananda before his demise wrote a letter to my Rangadadu in Rangoon to allow my didi ma and her family members to be at his ashram at Sargachi. The permission was given spontaneously. They had been to Sargachi for a few days. My mother got a golden chance to nurse and serve Swami Akhandananda. He would address my mother as "Rasabari" affectionately. I got all information from my mother when I was a student of Class II. When they took their departure from him, Swamiji was very grave and was seated on an armchair. During their stay at Sargachi he told them, "You will live long and experience *lilas* (divine and astounding activities) of Thakur (very likely he meant Sri Ramakrishna).

2

The World War II started within a few years and the world was shaken and ransacked. Man does not understand that he has got no right to spoil the world at his whims and caprices. For our foolishness we crucified Jesus and recently we find the Talibans destroying relics of Bamiyan Buddha. My grandfather's family along with my mother's reached Calcutta and within two days Swami Akhandananda left the mortal world. He was brought to Belur Math just twenty-four hours after the departure of Dadu's family and his sacred body was kept at Belur Math. My Ranga dadu and didi ma went to have a look and cried and cried. "Lila, Gurudeva was lying like Gautam Buddha" told my didima to my mother. In the biography of Swami Akhandananda the reference of the arrival of my didi ma and her children are given. As a matter of fact, my mother accepted Swami Akhandananda as her Gurudev too though she did not take initiation from him.

I was lucky that two best relatives of our family were my guardians now. I was really craving for this love and affection since childhood, but only after my Masters and during the unemployment phase, I was able to be with Ranga dadu and didi ma.

Everyone had a negative sympathy for me when I was caretaking the renovation of the building. My Ranga dadu and my didi ma were the exceptions. Ranga dadu was a brilliant scholar from Barisal BM College. His principal was Mr Nityalal Mukherjee, a first class in MA English. He was fashionable and extremely handsome. My trial as a caretaker was on and I forgot all my past memories, that I was the third son of NC Sharma, I forgot Paramjit, Kamal Kishore, Tasneem Dubey. I only desperately tried to survive. A few months after my Sunder mama came from England to attend the wedding ceremony of Kutti, I was overwhelmed to receive his family and his newly born baby boy, Dev Kumar at the airport. Kutti was born in Shimla during the tenure of World War II. Ranga dadu was posted in Shimla after he came back from Rangoon. Rangoon was ravaged by tremendous onslaught of the Japanese under Marshal Tojo. My didima became frail and failed to nurse her youngest boy. He was looked after by my mother.

My mother also reached from Pakhanjore with my sister and youngest brother. The condition of my mother's health was worsening and she told me, "You must accompany me when we go back to Pakhanjore." Sunder mama was scheduled to reach Calcutta on 23rd January, 1977 on a British Airways flight. On the previous day, I left Uttarpara with my youngest brother and the only son of my baro mama to stay in Gangulibagan for a night to reach the airport next morning with my mashis (my mother's sisters) and other family members. I made these plans lest my journey to the airport might get cancelled by my baro mama.

It was a cold night. We huddled together at my aunt's house. We reached airport early in the morning, almost everyone from Uttarpara including didima went. The flight landed right on time. As they came out after security check, they waved and nodded at everyone, but not with me or my youngest brother. We both were individually trying to draw their attention. But failed. They returned home in the hired private cars and me with my cousin and brother took the local train. When I reached Ranga Dadu's house, Sarada Niketan, I found my father was also there, relaxing on a cot. He had arrived that morning from Pakhanjore. My didima invited him to the marriage as a token of courtesy, but we never imagined he would attend the marriage function. I got upset seeing my so called unsophisticated, poor father among the so-called sophisticated relatives.

"Ha – What an excellent health you have developed my sunny!" said my father, seeing me entering in a very shattered state. I touched his feet without pleasure and he expressed his blessings silently. The previous day I had rushed to reach Dumdum in order to get sheepish grins from England returned relatives, but the very next day I was received with hundred percent genuine love and smile from a father who had somehow come from the wild forests of Dandakaranya Refugee Project.

"Let us go back to Pakhanjore together. If you stay here any longer, you will die. Calcutta is never a good place for us to live in," my father told me. I did not reply. I was trying to avoid a conversation with him in fear that I might be hijacked by him to Pakhanjore. Despite mounting pressure of laborious work for the preparation of the said marriage, I had been trying to snuggle up to my England returned mama and was very meticulously avoiding my father. I even sometimes tried to avoid my mother. They were neither urbanized nor sophisticated in the eyes of my glamorous relatives. Today they are no longer in this world. Sometimes I feel like shouting, shaking off all the stars of the universe to get them back once again…

The marriage ceremony took place on 24th January 1977. It was a pompous affair and also fascinating. My Ranga dadu and didima always paid attention to me in spite of the arrival of others. One evening both my father and England returned mama were discussing about me.

"He is whimsical, capricious, moody and listens to none," told my father.

"Yes, though I didn't talk to him regarding his career, but I understood he has no focus or aim. It is just meaningless on his part to while away his time," commented my Sunder mama.

I heard and told Kutti about it. He did not want me to go back to the DNK Project with my parents. In fact, whatever my father assessed about me was correct. Sunder mama told Kutti, "How long will you allow him to have his meals every day for nothing?" All these discussions were happening in my presence. I felt extremely insulted and humiliated and went straight to my Ranga dadu and asked, "Ranga dadu have you been feeding me meaninglessly? Did I not do anything for you? Don't you see my emaciated body like a beggar?" I angrily expressed my feelings.

"No, no, don't react. You have been toiling for months to get everything done perfectly in our family. Don't be so sentimental. There's a definite misunderstanding somewhere," he replied. He was a man of great personality. He spoke to my England returned mama. On interrogation my mama told, "I did not utter comments like this exactly, I was prejudiced by jamai babu."

The function for the marriage was over. All relatives who came for the occasion started returning. My father for one reason or another decided to go back to Pakhanjore alone. Meanwhile Sunder mama went back to England with his child and wife. I went along with my other relatives to Howrah Station to see off my father. I was insincere, casual and moved about aimlessly despite my failing career. Before the train left the station my father told me, "Why are you staying in Calcutta, at the cost of health and dignity? You should have gone back home with us. I am on the brink of retirement. Your mother's health is failing, your mejda has got married and your dada works on a meager salary in the South Suburban Municipality. Still you are whiling away your valuable time." His last statement failed to motivate me positively.

My dream to know the 'Captive Lady' was increasing despite my mounting problems. I had a firm conviction that in one way or the other I would get my Helen of Troy. I adore two regal ladies from the pages of World History. Cleopatra, the Empress of Egypt and last descendant of Ptolemy, ruler of Egypt nominated by Alexander the Great; and Noorjehan, the queen of Jehangir the Mughal emperor. I read the biography of Napoleon Bonaparte and marveled with the portrait of Marie Louisa, his queen. I did not believe that I was simply born to do mundane jobs, rather my purpose in life was to create an impactful change. My problems and ambition ran hand in glove. Today the dimension of my ambition has changed entirely. Back in 70s, dreams were the only resort to allow me to swim across the sea of my never-ending problems.

Within a few months of Kutti's marriage, I was re-employed in the same departmental store where I worked previously. Incidentally my health was shattered and clothes were tattered. I joined back. I disliked it but I had no choice. In 1977, Mrs Gandhi and the Congress party were defeated. Janata Party, under the leadership of Jay Prakash Narayan brought about the change in the Lok Sabha Election. Morarji Desai was chosen as the Prime Minister at a gathering in Rajghat by Jay Prakash Narayan and Acharya JB Kripalini. In West Bengal, Left Front led by CP(I)M formed government. Siddhartha Sankar Ray was removed and Jyoti Basu filled in the blank. Consequently, in the book stalls of Calcutta and West Bengal, Communist literature, books, magazines, journals were available in abundance. I started buying books on communism, socialism, revolutions of Lenin, history of Chinese liberation, long march of Mao Ze Dong. I was a voracious reader and despite my meager salary, I spent a lot on books. I was extremely impressed by a book on Chairman Mao written by Edgar Snow. But I never accepted the ruthless butchery by Communist China. I was swaying between the ideologies of violence and non-violence.

3

That year, some well-known Naxal leaders participated in the democratic election. Around the world a lot of things were happening. In the USA, Gerald R Ford, the President of Republican Party was defeated by Democrat Jimmy Carter in the presidential election. Zulfiqer Ali Bhutto, Prime Minister of Pakistan was arrested at midnight by Zia ul Haque, the military chief of Pakistan. Leonid Breznev became the omnipotent man of erstwhile USSR and simultaneously Ayatollah Khomeni of Iran came back to Tehran from Paris in 1979. There was a major shift in world politics. I was an ordinary salesman in a saree shop, yet failed to control my passion to do something great. I expressed my views to my friends, who were all junior to me at Uttarpara. They loved me, listened to me and laughed at me. My father saw caliber in every student. My mother discovered eternal goodness in all her children. But my father was analytical about our characteristics, so were my friends at Uttarpara.

I asked a friend Simanta, "Can't we start a radical movement like Russia or China? Can't we plunge into an international movement like Che Gue Vera did? Will nobody be able to emerge as Lenin or Mao?" I seldom liked Gandhi. "No at least not from Uttarpara," my friend returned in a cold voice. "Then why do you simply read 'Red Books' and communist literature? Do you just want claps from your friends over any argument?" I asked being annoyed.

It was evening. We four friends sat by the Birla Road, which runs from Makhla to Hind Motor. They did not pay much attention to me.

Many years ago, when my father graduated from BM College of Barisal, he nurtured an imagination to be a sannyasi under the aegis of Ramakrishna Mission. He came to Calcutta and one evening went to Belur Math. A saffron clad sannyasi was strolling on the bank of the Ganges. My father stood in the way, the Swamiji got irritated and asked, "Why are you standing in my way?"

"I just want to talk to you," he replied.

"I am not prepared today to waste my time for you," replied the sannyasi.

My father got disillusioned and came back. I similarly got gradually disillusioned with my dream to launch a movement like that of Russia and China. It is definite that my father's dream of becoming a sannyasi of Ramakrishna Mission or my vision to be a revolutionary to free the nation from its long-cherished maladies failed. I fail to understand why my father did not reach any spiritual height though he had saintly and magnetic personality. Meanwhile, my mother planned to come to Calcutta along with my only sister to fix up her nuptials. One evening I came back from The Departmental Store where I worked and saw my mother and sister at Ranga dadu's house. I had been staying there for almost two years now. I was delighted but could not enjoy their arrival as they had come permanently and I would have to undergo serious financial crisis. Due to prolonged poverty, I lost my glamour. My attire was usually worn out and old and the pair of shoes I wore was repaired several times. My father's pair of shoes was repaired till the mid-seventies and he had bought them in mid-sixties.

In 1972 Kutti went to Pakhanjore. The only doctor of Pakhanjore was our distant relative and we were invited to attend an evening tea meet. My mother reached there in a tattered pair of slippers and my mama asked, "Has didi got no better slippers?"

"No," I said.

Next morning my mama bought a pink plastic slipper for my mother from the local market. Meanwhile, dad retired, Khadu bhai fathered a daughter on July 2, 1977. My mother finding no choice reached Kolkata with my only sister. I continued reading communist literature and was moved by the epical life of Mao, impressed with the phenomenal political struggle of Lenin. I wanted to be like them. "Yes, I want to be like them. Do you have any objection?" I asked my baro mama, at the dining table.

"Think about your own future. Don't be riddled with reverie," he replied.

"But none can prevent me from joining a movement if there be any likewise," I retorted. My Ranga dadu brought the fire of argument under control. Still, I was hallucinated with violent political ideas and idols. Later when I shifted to Parnasree in Behala, I came across Tamosha and fell in love with her, I was tired of not being able to love anybody. I had never approached any girl before I met her. I was also irritated by my dull and painful service in the Departmental Store. One morning I reached the shop on time and found it closed. I ran to the main office of the proprietor and asked, "Sir! Why is the shop closed?"

"It has badly flopped," Prabir da replied.

I asked, "Sir what should I do now?"

"You may join again the post of street salesman on commission basis," he replied. I walked from Gariahat to Chetla and met baro mama. He was then working in the budget department of Damodar Valley Corporation. I applied for the post of a peon on temporary basis. The sky was overcast with dark clouds, a storm was brewing in the horizon. Then it started raining and I got drenched. I boarded a bus and reached Parnasree where I found my home locked. I had no choice but to go to the house of my jyathamosai. The second son of my jyathamosai shouted, "Hurrah! You have got an appointment letter. Immediately you have to join New Alipore Multipurpose School as an Assistant Teacher of English on deputation vacancy."

I was overwhelmed with a flow of indescribable emotion. I went through the appointment letter and heaved a sigh of relief. A span of respite from pain and drudgery at last! Before joining school, I felt perturbed. I was never a good student, though I somehow managed to pass all exams. New Multipurpose School at that time was one of the best Bengali medium schools of Calcutta. I joined, I taught, I conquered and the last date in that school was gradually approaching. I spoke to Pradip Chakraborty, a Bengali teacher in that school who knew Sulekha Goswamy, the Principal of St Joseph and Mary's School. It was not a board recognised school then and consisted of about 300 students.

"Follow me," told Pradip da, "and never utter a single Bengali word when I introduce you to Mrs Goswamy." I followed him, reached the school and did not utter a single word in Bengali. The school was in New Alipore and was run by Mrs Goswamy though it was founded on January 16, 1963 by Mr TL Lumb, a roving European leather technologist.

"Write an application immediately," told Mrs Goswamy.
I replied, "Ma'am I am not prepared to write any application right now."

She said, "Come with your application tomorrow."

I did likewise and the date of interview was fixed. I was asked by Mrs Goswamy to prepare 'We are Seven' of William Wordsworth. Before I reached a class and faced the students to teach them before the members of the interview board, she came out and told me to teach another chapter. I was extremely perturbed and expressed my inability to teach from a new chapter. "Oh, you have already prepared! Don't worry," told Mrs Goswamy, she was my mother surrogate. I went inside, saw the students, got nervous and made a mess.

You see Charlie, I had not totally conversed in English before that. Thankfully I got the appointment letter and joined on February 2 ,1979, about 21 years before my father's demise. I came to be known as BS Sir. There were many beautiful lady teachers but I did not dare approach any. I was the junior most teacher in the school with a total emolument of Rs 420. I suffered from an inferiority complex for my half rural background. Mrs Goswamy tried her best to help me get rid of this unintelligent psychological infringement. I improved a lot but my lack of introspection was killing me, I paid more attention to improve my English accent than other aspects. On silent nights, I stared at the glittering stars of a dark sky. Trees stood like mute spectators. I felt an external power in me to shake off the globe. I failed to measure it. I wept in silence, but did not feel comfortable Charlie, my dear.

Chapter 7
Life as a Principal

1

Democrats were ruling USA and Jimmy Carter was the President. The Indian government run by Janata Party was unsuccessful. Mrs Indira Gandhi returned to power with a landslide victory. James Callaghan of Labour Party in England was defeated by Conservative Party and Margaret Thatcher became the Prime Minister. Shah of Iran went absconding with Sahbanu Farah Diba and his family. Ayatollah Khomeni installed a new government under Abul Hassan Bani Sadr. A crisis between Iran and Iraq of Saddam Hussein started for Sat ul Arab. Zulfikar Ali Bhutto was hanged, the President of Bangladesh was ripped with bullets and killed in Chittagong. Red Army of USSR entered Afghanistan and posed Babruk Karmal as President. Hua Kuo Feng was removed from China and Teng Hsio Ping had the charge of the country. Entire globe was changing rapidly. But soon Carter became unpopular, facing the worst onslaught from Iran, for Iran had more than one hundred American hostages. They were released after receiving enormous indemnity. The world was burning with violent conflagration of fools who ran the governments. Being incompetent to solve any problem they resorted to destruction and violence.

I did not leave my conventional track of life. I plunged into a love affair with Tamosha. She was almost my age, dark complexioned with long hair and big, romantic eyes. On February 6 of '79, she took off from Kolkata for Dehradun with her mother, youngest sister and her grandmother. I went to Howrah Station to see them off. On 11th February a telegram reached her second sister "Mother expired this morning. Jain Dharamshala, Dehradun." Then and there I arrived at a conclusion to marry her. There was mild objection from my highly cultured mother and my erudite father. I turned a deaf ear. I went to the Marriage Register office at Hazra and got our marriage registered. My life was changing rapidly just as the world was worsening rapidly too.

After the death of Pandit Jawaharlal Nehru, the vibration of shock throughout the nation made me feel it was an achievement in becoming great in every aspect of life. In the early 80s, I was mesmerized with the astounding and phenomenal personality of Mrs Indira Gandhi. But today I am able to discover far stronger and super human geniuses like Mahatma Gandhi, Martin Luther King (Junior), Patrice Lumumba, Che Guevera or Nelson Mandela.

Anyway, a day after my marriage, I was walking along Lake Road with my wife and asked, "Do you really love me or you had no alternative, so you chose to marry me?" She did not reply. "You definitely love Amlan of your office more than me, or Ashish who stays in our locality." Still she did not reply. It was dusk and we both were walking silently. I was getting very angry. Once again it seemed that my effort and hopes remained unfulfilled. Amlan's influence on Tamosha was hard to forget. We went to Kashmir in 1981 with some office friends and the celestial beauty of the valley amazed me. But I am still astounded with the mysterious proportion of love Tamosha exhibited for me in Kashmir. During the entire tour, I quarreled with her and surrendered every time. "Are you mad?" she hurled angrily. "It's your fault!" I replied. "Do you want to spoil my life?" she said. "Yes!" I returned. "You may go," she said. "Yes, but before that I must destroy you," I replied. Wild extremism always existed, even in the best time and always in the worst of our love affair.

We returned from Kashmir with a heavy heart and ecstasy. The long mountainous route from Jammu to Kashmir is just incredibly exciting. Its beauty was melodious, waterfalls were sonorous. I enjoyed it thoroughly. Twenty years ago, Tamosha did not love me, yet I married her and my imagination of Henrietta crumbled to dust. I did not know why. My attraction for Henrietta was for a peculiar reason. I believed in any kind of work for world unification she would be the best person at the helm. But she made a fool of me, she was selfish. I am a half happy family man with my only child. I felt very much like John Lennon. He composed an excellent song after the birth of his first son. Really my son at that time was the most precious gift, my only solace. I jumped in joy at the hospital when I first saw him, he looked like an angel with jet black hair, pink complexion, red lips and beautiful eyes.

I wanted to live in the world for thousand more years. My son was growing up beautifully. "Ma, how will he be?" I asked my mother. "A great one," she replied. "Will he be handsome; will he be rich?" I asked. My mother replied, "Que sera sera, what will be will be, the future is not ours to see." After his birth USSR collapsed, the Gulf War took a diabolical shape, but could not culminate into a global catastrophe.

On September 2001, around 9am planes hijacked by the terrorists crashed into World Trade Centre in USA and thousands were killed in a minute. The news shook the globe, were we really heading towards doomsday? Who will save us? Mediocre politicians of the world are responsible in making the world a hecatomb. After World War II when efforts were launched to change the planet into a better one, super power race ignobly concocted sporadic chaos in the globe. I believe America is the *avante garde* to allow terrorism to achieve international dimension. International terrorists these days are running parallel underground governments. Today America and civilians of America are the worst victims of American Government's child play for more than half a century.

I became the Principal of my school on 11th February 1993. On February 11, 1996, Gideons from Europe and America came to visit our school and offered me beseeching to convert to Christianity. In many respects 11th of every month in one way or the other is important to me. On one such date, I was sitting alone in a dark room when Henrietta came to me.

"What do you want to do with me?" I asked her.

"Nothing, your frustration for everything forced me to come to you," she replied.

"What will you do with me? Get me rid of frustration? You are selfish, shrewd, peevish and unfit even to utilize your own brilliance," I told her.

"Wherever I can be, whatever your conclusion about me may be, I am always with you and I will always be with your, all globetrotting programmes and projects."

"I care a fig for your effeminate sympathy. I am not a baby from your womb," I shouted at her. "You never tried to understand me and that's my worst tragedy. Will you be off and allow me to contemplate over the recent disasters in America?

I'm really awaiting a global change and it's not possible without American plunge. I've got no time to spend romantically with you. It's a critical juncture. Please go away, let me concentrate to fulfill my mission. I've already wasted years for you. I need to go forward to show the world a new path, a new dream, a new dimension," I replied.

"Why do you consider yourself to be an extra ordinary superman? You can just be a better principal than you are today. You even cannot love without response. Great prophets loved man without expectations and you talk like a prophet meaninglessly," she replied.

"I never wanted to be a prophet with you, Henrietta!" I retorted furiously. "Please do go away and never come back again. I have not been born for you. I have been born for mankind. I am here to be the pioneer of the world. I'm here to save the world from collapse and destruction." I returned. And she left. I was in a stupor.

"Henrietta," I shouted like a mad man.

When I reached home late, Tamosha was angry. I straightaway went to bed. I woke early dawn, went to the verandah, millions of stars were glittering in the sky. I wanted to spend my whole life with this heavenly silence.

The woods are lovely, dark, and deep,
But I have promises to keep,
And miles to go before I sleep,
And miles to go before I sleep.
(Stopping by the Woods on a Snowy Evening by Robert Frost)

Gradually a new day dawned. The sun lit the sky like waves, in the dancing universe, the world is nothing but a toy. Why should we bother for America, why should we bother for Osama bin Laden,

"So-aham, so-aham, so-aham, Shiva-aham,Shiva-aham,Shiva-aham !"

2

As a retaliation to the terrorist attack in USA, George Bush lodged an attack on the Talibans, to catch hold of Osama bin Laden. Meanwhile, I had to go to New Delhi with Tamosha. I reached the airport just eight minutes before departure of the flight. Next morning at 10.30am we reached Shajahan Hall of Taj Continental Hotel to attend a conference. I was the last speaker. I had no choice but to state, "I am neither a celebrity nor an actor. I am neither a politician, minister nor any well-known personality of the world. I cut a sorry figure when I find that men of this planet Earth want to be lions, tigers, dogs. Man does not want to be a man in the real sense of the term. Until man tries to be a man, there will be repetition of nuclear bombs like Hiroshima, Nagasaki. There will be destructions of World Trade Centre buildings of New York and explosions in Pentagon. We are mentally bankrupt and misled. I am also in no way free from that infection. So, we have to think about the welfare and development of the globe in a changed dimension."

In my lecture I referred that 42% population of India still live below international poverty line. "Billions in the world are still in penury. The governments of the world are responsible for every kind of crisis. We, the mankind must resort to a united effort to form a global government or a super state structure of government to allow man to get better opportunities to live like humans on this planet. We must run a spiritual global movement to save the world from inevitable collapse. Anyway, I thank you very much for paying attention to an important speech of an unimportant person like me."

Surprisingly my speech was much applauded. Mr. Arnold came to me and I got down from the dais and he embraced me. "My son, everyone speaks in favour of the system, none dares to openly criticize it. You dared to open up in a conference," he told me. Miss Arnold came with her mother. I touched their feet. They reminded me of my parents. After returning to Calcutta, I came to know from my colleague C. Das, that some students of his class will agitate against Mr Roy Chowdhury for beating some students. "You are the class teacher; don't let them do it. You will have no chance to get rid of the allegation of creating a furore by the students" I said

"Sir, I don't care. I am hundred percent genuine from the core of my heart," he said.

"But I don't believe that students are going to do something without your guidance," I replied.

I reached school next morning and was welcomed with posters and placards. Mr C Das was an ex-student of the school and now was a teacher, one of the youngest teachers of the school. I believed he was the mastermind behind this agitation. The students were all candidates for the forthcoming ICSE board exams. There were teachers who were dedicated ones like Nibedita Dutta, who became integral part of the institution. Her attractive personality and versatility delighted me but she later decided to move to USA for her masters and research work. She even got my interview published in the newspaper. I borrowed a book from her, a book written by Jhumpa Lahiri. "I'm not dying today. I must leave an eternal piece of work for man. Don't dare count my age. I'm stronger than a teenager," that's what I told her.

She however replied: "Please Sir, I'm tired of your reverie and hallucinated ideas. Get rid of that and leave me. Your dream is an El Dorado. I have a fixed destination. I'm not fool enough to spoil my life for your scheme of building castle in the air."

Charlie do you know, I formed an organization 'World Unification League' with all male members and boys. It was registered but crashed at the take off stage. Thenceforth I tried to start a movement with female members. Tamosha did not like it. In course of my day-to-day work pressure, I forgot my friends, associates and companions, trying to run much ahead of my time and plunge into my imaginary world. I did not feel like going back to civilization of Egyptian Pharaohs, but a wish to stand in front of Tutankhamen, Ramses I and Nefertiti. I felt that I was the Sphinx, I was the colossal statue. I was in search of them not in the pages of history but in the distant chasm of my innermost mind like a hallucination. I enjoyed my journey through the deserts of Sinai like Moses, could hear the clarion call of the Nile, the trumpeting of the deserts of Arabia. But how will I help in awakening the dormant world? I could not decide whether Henrietta would be able to be the principal partners of my movement. I said to myself. "They are for themselves. They are keen on decorating their lives like average ladies of the world do. They neither are Nefertiti or Cleopatra nor Noorjehan." They lacked dreams.

Soon I got a call to attend a seminar in Hyderabad. This was after the one where I received the 'Indira Gandhi Excellence Award' from his excellency Mr Bhisma Narayan Singh and Mr GVG Krishnamurthy. This time I was called upon to deliver a speech on Mother Teresa, and I had no preparation. Some of her books were in my bag when I boarded the plane. During the short flight, I read as much as I could and tried to remember the minute details. I was accompanied by my wife, son, Mr Chatterjee and Mrs Sinha. Next afternoon I reached Hotel Viceroy located near Hussein Sagar Dam. I heard a discussion in the audience that the main speaker on Mother Teresa was coming from Calcutta. I did not realize that they were talking about me! My name was announced first to occupy a seat on the dais. I spoke on Mother Teresa. My oration was much applauded.

The award ceremony was over. I got down from the dais and was surrounded by many from the audience. "Sir, where do you stay in Calcutta?" asked a lady Principal of some college.

"Sir are you a Principal of a school or college?" asked another.

"Sir, please stand with us for a photograph," a young handsome gentleman requested.

In Hyderabad they forgot that I was not a celebrity. In Delhi the matter was always a bit different. I just had a cup of tea and hurried off to see the statue of Lord Buddha on Hussein Sagar. My son who accompanied me, had a carbuncle and he was in a lot of pain, so I failed to see the statue of Lord Buddha. In 1983, I had been to this city for the first time, to bring back my wife from Uppal. She went there for a short training course for two months. I went to Hyderabad again in 2001 with my family and colleagues. During my visit in 1983, I managed to drag Tamosha to reach the top of the Golkonda Fort. I had my friend Mr Rajiv Sharma with me. He was also a trainee from New Delhi to Uppal.

"Rajiv, where shall we have our meal after visiting the fort?" I asked him.

"Kahin bhi kha lenge, pehle isko dekh to leyn (We will have our meal somewhere but first let us see the fort)." Sheikh Akhtar was our guide. "Saab jab agle bar yahan ayenge to mera hi naam puchhiyiega (Ask for me when you come the next time)."

In the short span of seventeen years, I didn't dare enquire about Sheikh Akhtar's whereabouts. I heard that Rajiv Sharma was killed by some terrorists in a bus on his way home to Punjab from Delhi. I still don't believe the news. But neither did I try to enquire, I was afraid of the authenticity of the rumour. I was missing both Sheikh Akhtar and Rajiv this time at Hyderabad. I had so many memories with them. Over years, I too changed, I am a father now, a Principal of the school which I joined as an assistant teacher. In front of the Golkonda Fort, I was thinking to myself, "Is Rajiv still alive? Where is Akhtar miyan? Is it the same Golkonda Fort? Is time really that powerful to wipe out everything?"

3

After returning to Calcutta, I plunged into a sea of work and I knew I had to cross it, however wide and taxing it might be. Meanwhile a letter reached me from The Telegraph to take part in 'Better Calcutta Contest.' We had 'Health Category' as our project. My colleagues organized camps for Polio vaccinations for slum children. Mrs S. Sen, the chief conductress of the project came to take a note of our camps. Polio vaccination was going on. She had three lieutenants for video recording. She was escorted to the chamber of the Principal where I was sitting. "Sir you have to have more involvement to bring about right sort of health awareness in the children. This Health Care Project is in fact for welfare of the poor and the have-nots of our society," she said.

"Yes, we need to do something for them." I also added that mere slum projects for a short span of time will give us reputation, fame, satisfaction and awards, but society will always remain just the same. In this world Buddha failed, Christ failed, Gandhi failed and I am sure there will be many more failure in future. I accompanied them to a nearby slum area which was our target to win the prize. I was a bit late. My colleagues were instructing our student volunteers to spray DDT, Phenol, and distribute mosquito coils to the slum dwellers. In fact, our children were experts in doing it. Our school had the largest Interact club in Asia.

I left my colleagues and Mrs Sen and told the students: "Follow me. Let us go further in." The students followed me blindly, without any hesitation. "There will be no slums," I extorted. My students, head over heels in joy began following me. I remembered Mother Teresa with devotion and trudged through the slum. Their toilets were in pathetic condition. There were drains of sorts but no proper drainage system. I met an elderly lady who lost her young son in 1999. She was behaving like a half mad woman. "Ma, I'm your son. Whenever you are in trouble let me know. Remember I will always be with you," I said, touched her feet and we were photographed. I again visited the slum and enquired about the elderly woman, but no one could give me information about her. As usual in all my visits I sprayed DDT, phenol, kerosene in the drains of the slum along with my dear students. They distributed mosquito coils. And the children of the slum started collecting them like hot cakes!

"Sir, we are not happy. Why do you ask the photographer to come with us?" asked Simi, a student of Class XI of the Commerce section who lived in the slum.

"We get ourselves photographed so as to make us more important, by blackmailing the poverty of the poor," I retorted.

In a massive gathering in the Science City Auditorium among remarkable Industrial plenipotentiary along with Mr Ranjit Modi, we were awarded the best prize in 'Health Category' in Better Calcutta Contest. It consisted of a huge trophy, a certificate, a gift cheque of Rs 2000/.

Chapter 8
My Love, Greta

1

There was a phase when I was rather confused, about my career run, who were my friends, about those who loved me and a whole lot of other views. Surprisingly, I discovered that I too did not love anyone without expectation. But was that the true case? When I left Nivedita and allowed her to go her way, I failed to sleep the whole night, even sedatives did not work.

I was going to Bangladesh on work and then to a seminar in Kathmandu. Apart from two flights a week, there were no direct flights from Calcutta to Kathmandu and had to reach Nepal via Dhaka. I woke up around 5am in the morning and got ready for the airport with Tamosha, my son and his friend. My son did not want to be in our boring company. So, he was allowed to stay back in Calcutta. He and his friend accompanied us to the airport to see us off. I boarded the flight with Tamosha and two more members of the team. It was a small plane.

Incidentally, this was the very Bangladesh that I left when it was East Pakistan, in February, 1964. From our village Batajore, I reached Barisal town on a bus. We had a brief stay in Alekanda, the hired house of my *sejo jyathamosai.* From there we availed a steamer; it was at the time of Hazratbal Riot. Next morning we reached Khulna, a train to India and reached via Petrapole and Benapole. I was taken to Dhaka by my parents in 1962, the year my father appeared for his MA Examination in English from the Dhaka University and his examination centre was Curzon Hall. After so many years, I was again travelling to Dhaka, this time with my wife. On the Bangladesh Biman flight everyone was conversing in Bangladeshi dialect. A passenger and one of the crew members had a haughty conversation for some inconveniences caused onboard. We reached Dhaka and was received by the Joint Secretary of Jute Department of Bangladesh who escorted us to the Secretary of Civil Aviation Department.

We were offered tea. "Did you come to Bangladesh before?" asked the official in Bangladeshi Bengali.

"No, I left East Pakistan in 1964 with my parents. I have come to Dhaka after 40 years. Field Marshal Muhammad Ali Ayub Khan was then President of Pakistan. Hazrat Bal Riot forced us to leave this country."

The others with me had never visited this country before. The high ranking official asked, "Do you belong to Barisal?"

"Yes," I replied.

"What was your father doing there?" he asked.

"He was a headmaster of 14 different schools of this country at different times."

"Had he ever been to South Barisal?" he asked.

"Definitely, he was at Dhulia Gobindapur High School, Kalishuri High School."

He asked, "Would you mind telling his name?"

"Mr Nirmal Chandra Sharma," I replied.

"Oh, my goodness, only for a super teacher like him there are eleven colleges at Bouphal sub-division," he said.

"Have you met my father?"

"No I heard of him," he said.

After reaching the hotel, I called my cousins and my aunt at Tallabagh, they were *sejo jyathamosai*'s family. My *jyatha* was an LMF Doctor. He stayed with his eldest daughter at Bagoora and was killed by the Razakars during Bangladesh Freedom Movement. We hired a cab after lunch and went to visit Curzon Hall. I remembered the voluminous portals of Curzon Hall forty years back. But I failed to revive that same hypnotism in me again. We visited the Medical College and then went to Tallabagh. The second daughter of my *sejo jyathamosai* opened the door. I met her after 42 years. We were all overjoyed and all cousins had a great time, remembering the golden old days. On our way back to the hotel almost at every signal, the cabs and other vehicles were cordoned off and chased by hordes of beggars. But in spite of it, the city's pomp and grandeur was beyond measure.

The world can be made a much better place to live in, if state boundaries are removed. But then who will bell the cat? The governments of the world are being run by a monolithic virus of 'Mediocrity' and 'Below Mediocrity'. Still Nationalistic leaders like Lincoln, Kamal Ataturk, Roosvelt, Kennedy, Yasser Arafat,

Patrice Lumumba and Nelson Mandela are free from that virus attack. We reached our hotel and met the Joint Secretary and our principal host. He was waiting to dine with us and his family that evening at his residence. We went in his car, "What is the condition of the rural areas of Bangladesh?" I asked him.

"Remarkably good in all respects," he replied.

"How can you say so," I asked. "I have read through the UN Report that the poorest people of the world are living in the rural areas of Bangladesh!"

"Rubbish," he protested. "All those reporters prepare their reports from 'Hotel Gulshan', the super most posh hotel in the super most posh area in Dhaka. We have got the best medical facilities in our city in the Indian sub-continent."

I was surprised that he didn't know that many super specialty hospitals of India are infested with Bangladeshi patients. It was preposterous to continue my argument with him. Next morning, we took off for Kathmandu. My seminar in Kathmandu was not a failure but was not successful either. My time of lecture was curtailed by sycophants and politicians. I returned to Calcutta and finally met Nivedita, recited with her "Rabbin Ben Ezra" of Robert Browning in our utter frustration

Grow old along with me!
The best is yet to be,
The last of life, for which the first was made:
Our times are in His hand
Who saith "A whole I planned,
Youth shows but half; trust God: see all, nor be afraid!"

2

Nivedita was diagnosed with a tumour in her uterus. Operating it meant, she would never be able to become a mother. So, she made a hasty decision to marry her boyfriend Sanket immediately. Sanket was in the Air Force. Thankfully, medicines improved her tumour remarkably. We were invited to her wedding, but I did not attend. She even conceived soon and was delighted. I was bewildered not because of her happily married settled life but for the void left after her marriage. Paradigm of my love always runs negatively at the end. I lost all my self-confidence after my spine operation (Anterior Cervical Micro

Discectomy) in Chennai. I temporarily lost my strength, my stamina, my dreams, imagination, courage, hope and everything. I could not walk properly due to weak post operation trauma. I felt like crying. I could not even shed my tears. Only the silent sky was my listener.

"Tell them I came, and no one answered,
That I kept my word."

I needed a friend desperately at that moment to share my trauma. I felt I was all alone, forlorn, sequestered, though my family members and Tamosha were affable and tried their best to get me back to form. They thought I was still strong, ambitious and positive, but they were wrong. My operation took seven odd hours for a wide variety of complications. The neuro surgeon's dexterity was applaudable. Clinically I was perfect but physical and mental challenges broke me, I had no strength to combat my weakness from within and even outside.

I went to Chennai for a checkup and returned with partial confidence and good health. Then came Greta in my life, like a gurgling fountain, haunting all my passions. Greta showed me the way, resorted to effort to regain my lost potentials. I began regaining myself, my hope, my passion for life. Greta was my fortune, my hope, my delight, my dream, my frustration, my pain, my burning sensation, my joy, my tears, smile and my pride.

"Greta, I was a blind fan of Greta Garbo. I dreamt of her many times. Do you dream of any like me?" I asked her.

"No," she returned. "I do not fancy being a facsimile of any Garbo."

"Greta, fifteen years ago you were not married and I was a bachelor. Would you have loved me enough to marry me?"

"Never, my father General Mukherjee would have never allowed me to marry a diaspora from East Pakistan. But I could have loved you."

"For the last 25 years, I have been dreaming of a unified world, a super state, a single world government and no militarism. Will you be my principal associate to run a global movement to fulfill my dreams and dreams of many citizens?"

"No, my father was a top army officer. I have my own ideologies."

"So was my father, but not a top one," I replied.

"Your father changed his profession, was discharged from the Air Force at the fag end of the World War II. My father retired as a General. Militarism is my romanticism, my dream, my love. I adore Napoleon Bonaparte."

"I adore him too, but Napoleon in St Helena Island at the last phase of his life adored Jesus, adored Prophet Mahomet as the greatest achievers of the world. Why don't we follow his later development?" I retorted.

"Please don't try to change well nurtured idea of militarism, war and its charm. It's a precious legacy I inherited from my late father. Sunder, are you satisfied with civil regulations of our country? In our legal department innumerable cases are lying pending. It might take hundreds of years to get them resolved. I still believe military is indispensable for our nation," she replied. "Greta will you smoke?" I offered her a cigarette. I lit one and she smoked. We walked together and reached my car. Then she told me: "Sunder you are a first rate fool. You think like a downright lunatic, learn to build a life like a man."

I got furious and I shouted while driving. I was in a shock. I was unable to drive, my hands shook, and my throat was parched. I was sweating even in the winter month of December. I could not drive, and looked at her. She was in tears, touched my fingers, and gripped my hand in hers. She stroked my hair and my head. She cried too. I could not drive any longer. She drove me back home that night. I lay on my sofa and slept and when I woke up, it was dawn. I opened my window; a few stars were still shining in the fading sky. I took a deep breath. My phone rang, it was Greta. "Sunder, after reaching my house last night, I have neither changed nor slept," she said. I did not reply.

She repeated, "Come to me, it's a beautiful dawn. We shall sit in my garden. The white roses in my garden are really charming." I sat on the sofa smoking and looking at a portrait made by my son. It had been there for three years. I never enjoyed the painting as I was doing then. My unscaled ambition, frivolous mood and dream to be the greatest did not allow me to spend a happy life with Tamosha and my family. She was always neglected by me.

I came back to the drawing room. I got bamboozled to see Greta on the sofa. I went and sat by her. She was still wearing last night's salwar kameez. Tamosha came out from the bedroom and sat on the chair opposite to Greta. None of us spoke and then Tamosha left us and closed the bedroom door.

"I will die, I will die," Greta uttered, and it was the first sentence I had from her since she came. I smiled. She stood up. I left her standing.

"Whole night I was waiting for you in my car here only. You are mine, you are only mine, don't leave me please," she was crying. "You will forget me immediately if Harjeet comes back," I said.

"O Sunder, don't talk about him, only you and me, none else Sunder, None. You are only mine and I am only yours." "Forget me not," she said again. I did not want to love any without service to the mother earth and man. I only love Tamosha and my son.

Greta loved a Maharashtrian classmate, Sameer, when she was in college and they wanted to marry. But her father, a conservative General did not agree. Greta loved him more than anything else in the world. Their long love affair had a fall after six years. Greta was quite tall, dark complexioned, agile, and attractive and her eyes were deep as an ocean. Now she seemed to be the only pole star of my life.

I once told her, "Greta, we shall work together to unify the globe into a single super state for our posterity to come."

"Is it possible? War is a romantic concept for man from the dawn of civilization. How will mankind throw away their well nurtured super romanticism and make the world a dull place?"

"War is a barbarous practice. I find no romanticism in killing humans. War creates more problems than it solves," I replied. We were walking in the Millennium Park.

"Rubbish! It's a part of our civilization. Have you forgotten the term 'War time footing?' Many discoveries of science were expedited and surfaced due to wars only. Without warfare theory of Malthus will be partially correct. War Technology is feeding millions. It is mathematics and science," she retorted.

"Do you welcome the destructive force of a tsunami, as it creates population balance in the world?" I asked her.

"Oh no! I am not at all that diabolic. Maybe it is a necessary evil of nature."

"Maybe it is a reaction of Nature against our abuses," I said.

"Why do you always think about the world and posterity? Just to be a famous historical giant?" she screamed.

"I will never be able to let you feel like me. I love this world. A man willingly can never be a giant or colossus of any type. Let all of us think over the 'Brief History of Time' by Prof Stephen Hawking. We shall definitely discover a new dimension for man for the world itself. I believe that the earth is the queen of the universe."

"My dear, all your dreams will just be a fiasco. There is no reason in it and sounds quite ridiculous," she said.

"My lord! colonialism, after hegemony and onslaught of terrorism came, there must be an onslaught for unification of the world and man. We have got nothing to lose but our chains. If suppression of man by conquering empires was necessary, so are colonialism, hegemony, terrorism and then unification of the world and man. It is a form of evolution."

My voice was a bit loud. Many visitors in the park looked at us in surprise. Greta remained silent. We walked together and she silently got in her car. I blindly followed her and she drove off with me. She knew the roads better and drove. We reached Bishop Lefroy Road where we got down. She reached a complex and took me to the fifth floor to her flat.

"It's my mother's flat. She has gone to Germany to visit my brother," she informed. She went inside and I sat blankly. Couple of minutes later, she came back with two cups of coffee. I gave her a cigarette. She lit it and I lit mine.

"I joined German classes in Max Mueller Bhavan and became friends with Ranen. He was thirty-nine and I was just twenty-one. He had just been divorced three months before and had a child. The child would go to meet his mother on Sundays. I used to meet Ranen on afternoons in his flat."

She next described at least six important years of her life in Ladakh. I stood up, leaving the coffee unfinished when she embraced me, kissed me randomly but I did not. She went on: "I was unable to forget Sameer, my first love, even after marriage. I cried before my husband and confessed everything. My husband promised that only once he would accompany me to Sameer's house."

But as Greta narrated about her male friends, I felt jealous. I did not want her simply for voluptuous joy. I loved her. I thought she would be a great partner to work on my mission for the world. "Greta, I will trace only Sameer, will escort you to him too. He was your first love. Probably the only person in the world you loved passionately. I can't hear your trauma any longer," I consoled her. I tried to tell her that I love her as a madman loves his madness, a tsunami loves its catastrophe, as the low ebb loves the high tide, the swan the lake, the birds the sky, the sun the solar family. But I failed to reveal my secret to her.

She continued: "One-night Harjeet came to me. It was 2am. He asked me to ride his motorbike and we rode off through silent mountainous roads. We both got down, walked through the silent, rough terrain, we left the main road. I followed him. The unmetalled road was undulating. We reached a small fountain. It was glittering in the moonlight. It was sometimes in January and the water of the fountain was ice cold. We played in that fountain in the early hours of the morning. He showered me with kisses. I too returned. We forgot the cold, forgot it was January, and forgot the world. In fact, we forgot everything. I reached home while Harjeet returned to his mess. I found my children crying and afraid. They cried in the silence of the night. They cried for not being able to find me when they had awakened. I was all wet. I cried too, embracing them."

While she narrated the incident to me, she was crying. I was overjoyed. I did not know the cause of my mystical pleasure on hearing Greta's confession. She continued her story, "Harjeet kept coming to my house in my husband's absence. My husband took off almost for a year to Kalaikunda for an official stint. Harjeet would come to our flat almost thrice a week. He was childish, younger to me by two years, tall and handsome. I went astray when Harjeet did not come. One day as I was strolling with my son, a South Indian officer came and propositioned me. He knew about my affair with Harjeet. I was a bit scared that he might disclose the incident to my husband when he returned. I hurried back agitated and nervous. I did not go outside my house for the next few days. One evening I went outside for a walk. The aged South Indian man came my way. That night he reached my house and tried to seduce me. I gave my children their dinner and told them that I had some work with the visitor. I went to the bathroom and cried. That night Harjeet came again. I cried in front of him and did not tell him anything about the visitor. I tolerated the insult in silence. I did not imagine in my wildest dream that I might get anyone to confess all of it," she finished. She was silent. I remained silent too. The dark pall of dusk was descending, and the sound of conch shells rang from afar.

3

It was raining outside and Greta dragged me to the corner of the bed in her mother's room. She forced me to lie down. I was tired and slept off. When I woke up it was 9 pm. I hurried away and left her in her mother's apartment. I believed that from tonight Greta would be a great partner of mine for Man and world unification. But Henrietta could have been a better partner for sure!

The following evening, I went to meet Greta in her mother's house. I told her everything regarding that storm in a tea cup, the harassment and insult that I had to undergo. She got upset. She hoped that the clouds of misfortune would dispel soon. Just to divert my mind, she began talking about all sundry matters. "Harjeet had three attractive photographs of mine and all were without a stitch. I telephoned him to give it back. But he asked me to go to Bangalore in June to collect them and get myself photographed again in the same pose and in the same manner. I feel like meeting him but I will not do that only for you," said Greta. I got puzzled. I did not know how to reply or what to reply.

"You should meet him if you loved him," I suggested.

"I feel like going to Bangalore in June but I choose to restrain my passion," she replied.

Restrain and she! "I will bear the expenditure of your journey. Love between you and Harjeet is a dormant volcano. Your next meeting will invite volcanic eruption. You will be euphoric, furiously delighted. Leave alone the matters of the photograph. That's an alibi to meet Harjeet."

She became furious and said, "Harjeet is a very good man and a sincere lover, possesses the best heart. I like you but I love him. I adore your qualities but I adore his goodness more. I can sacrifice everything for him."

I did not know what to say. I sweated, took a deep breath and left. Reaching home, I asked Tamosha to get the VCD of 'Chokher Bali' of Tagore. It was directed by Rituporno Ghosh. I tried to divert my mind from Greta and concentrate on the film. Suddenly the light went off. Again, apparition of Greta and Harjeet arrived in front of me. I just could not get rid of that. I had a glass of whisky with ice. It burnt my body and soothed my mind. I felt very bad for Tamosha. Suddenly the light was on. The VCD started from where it had stopped and I watched the movie. But I felt like resigning myself to silence. I decided that from the next day onwards I would definitely go to our garden house at Diamond Harbour very frequently for respite and rest. Tamosha and my son shall go with me.

Chapter 9
My Pillars of Strength

1

My Dear Charlie
I got disgusted and wished to leave Calcutta. I went on a tour to entire South India with my family, three colleagues and their families, Kanyakumari, her husband, Deb Kumar and daughter. Deb was an IT executive and along the entire trip was busy with his official work and my wife was busy with the wives of my colleagues. We reached Kanyakumari i.e. Cape Commorin. I and Kanyakumari went for a stroll along the beach.

"What was your instant feeling when you saw Masima's (my mother) dead body in the morning?" she asked me.

"*E kon sakal, rater cheye andhakar* (this morning is darker than the darkest night). My tongue was parched, my head reeled, and I heard a volcanic sound. I was not only flabbergasted, I was undone," I returned.

"When were you the happiest?" she asked again.

"I am still waiting for the moment," I returned.

"Why do you want to crumble everything for world unification?"

"I don't know. I love it only," returned I.

The waves were breaking at the shore incessantly, for centuries, the sea has been roaring, from dawn of civilization or perhaps even before that. It has been roaring probably when there was no life on earth, from the beginning of time. It will be roaring till the end of time. Kanyakumari's daughter was running and playing on the beach. We were walking and walking. This journey had no end. During my sojourn with Kanyakumari, I discovered she was selfish, ruthless and muddleheaded. It was difficult to tolerate her whims and moods. She got irate seeing me and Tamosha together.

"My father sacrificed his life for the cause of education of the poor Muslim students in the erstwhile East Pakistan and Namosudras in India's Dandakaranya Refugee Project. In East

Pakistan he worked under competent bureaucrats and in the DNK Project, the bureaucrats were first class idiots. While in India, we were in abysmal poverty and my father was optimistic of one world government. He neither lost his health nor his hope. An unparallel man," I told.

Kanyakumari was walking. I could not understand if she was listening. "My father was an Additional Secretary in Food Department," she returned after five minutes. Her mobile phone rang. She said: "We have to return. Tamosha and Deb are waiting for us with breakfast." We began walking back silently. Her daughter was the exception. We were nearing the hotel.

"My father had no recognition from any social corner. I always brood over this." She didn't reply.

The long walk ultimately had a dull end. Reaching the hotel, I took a bath and returned to the breakfast table. "Sir, the tea is getting cold," Kanyakumari said. We were seated. It was around 7 am. I was tired after my long walk. The tea rejuvenated me.

"Sir," Kanyakumari told, "You are obsessed with your father, aren't you?"

"In 1977 my father came to Calcutta from Pakhanjore of Dandakaranya. My mother, sister, and the youngest brother had come earlier. My father was retiring and he needed support for his family. None of his children were competent to give him solace. My mother had the worst health. Dad boarded the Bombay Mail to reach Raipur so that he could avail the bus for Pakhanjore and his traumatic condition and poor health did not have any impact on me," I said.

"It's very natural. You were too young to feel your father's trauma," Tamosha returned.

I was sipping tea. "My father expired on 3rd February, 2000. Sunder Mama was in Calcutta for a brief sojourn with a theatre team of Tagorians from England. Next morning he reached. I tried to start to converse about my father, *Sunder mama* chatted about the theatre group. I was in tears. He failed to see my face. He was asking about how many passes we might need to reach Rabindra Sadan as audience for his show from Great Britain was on 11th February, sixteen hours after we burnt our father. It increased my trauma. God! Was he not able to fathom our condition after my father's death from a sudden and massive heart attack?"

I felt my father's breathing, I smelt his fragrance. Everyone was sitting in a hushed atmosphere, relaxing on the verandah. I was keen on speaking incessantly about my father. Probably none was that keen to listen. Mr Nair, chemistry teacher of our school was the only keen listener. I apprehended this from his curious eyes. Only he broke the ice, "Sir, we heard that your father was a short-tempered man with profuse physical strength and you were rigorously beaten up by him. You would get irate and expressed anger to your mother, but you did not. Didn't you have delicate feelings for him during your boyhood?"

I started, "My father got employed in SS Memorial High School in Odisha as Headmaster under the administrative periphery of DNK Refugee Project. It was 1965, February. We boarded the Up Bombay Mail from Howrah in the forenoon. My *Rangadadu*, *Baramama* , *Kuttimama* and *Baradadu* were in the station to see us off. Everyone, other than my father was crying. It was outrageously shocking when my *Rangadadu*, a dignified old man with Roman emperor like personality was pressing his face with a stark white handkerchief to control his outburst. After coming from Bangladesh, we were sheltered in his house. My father was jobless. My godlike *Rangadadu* took up all our responsibility including our schooling for almost a year. I have seldom met a person like him. He was crying and so was everybody. My father was glum but happy, for he could get his own family back again.

The following day we reached Raipur. Bhabaranjanda of Kachchipara (my birthplace) of Barisal received us. He was ITI instructor at Mana Camp. It was a tedious journey of five hours. Reaching Kondagaon we changed the bus for Umerkote that trudged through dense forest. Roads were hilly and undulating and locals were mostly *adivasis*. It was dusk, my father sat in a remote corner of the bus. He wore a white shirt and black trousers, and was bespectacled. I felt what if my father died in this dejected forlorn place! A strange fit of passion enveloped me. The bus was running, the forest was dark and enigmatic. I sobbed, none saw me. I was eleven years old and was crying silently as I feared father's death in this Godforsaken land.

I felt nothing for my loving mother or my brothers and only sister. Twenty-one years later, I reached Dandakaranya to bring my father back to Calcutta. He died in 2000. No, I did not let my 'Ozymandias' die in Dandakaranya."

Much later I remember talking with my father and one of my colleagues regarding litigations of our school. Suddenly Baba told, "I will go to your school tomorrow and spend time with your children." He then went to the washroom and I decided not to allow him to call on my students at such a critical juncture. My father came back, my colleague expressed the official inconvenience in escorting my father to school. "Okay I shall not go, I will not disturb you." He was shocked but it did not have any impact on me. I did not change my decision. I have been repenting it after his death.

Nair said: "Tell us something about your mother."

2

"My mother had an extraordinary character. A protagonist of a battle where she was vanquished and ransacked. She was a brilliant student when she was in Rangoon (Yangon), religious, sophisticated, agile, enlightened, tall and beautiful. But she had become emaciated, skinny, dry, handicapped, and helpless at the time of her death. She saved my father from many impending dangers in East Pakistan. At the cost of her health and comfort, she made us healthy. She was the most precious asset in her father's family. They were simply diasporas from Burma (Myanmar). Her outstanding brilliance, indomitable courage, phenomenal spirits were our respite during our stay in the most backward places of the sub-continent in downright poverty.

Most of father's students in East Pakistan addressed my mother as 'Ma'. Once she had four pieces of bangles only and she gave two pieces to the daughter of our poor village *pandit mahasaya.* She adored Subhash Chandra Bose and revered Swami Akhandananda the most. When I came to my hostel during my HS, I used to cry for my mother, but did not shed a single drop when she died. She was not imaginative like my father. They were diametrically opposite in their personality and their constant bickering spoiled them and tortured us. She told me stories of 'Les Miserable' of Victor Hugo and 'Jean Christophe' of Romain Rolland.

My mother was given no proper care, proper treatment and nursing during the span of her prolonged ailment. Once I got angry with my youngest brother, we were about to fight, my mother came to stop any kind of tussle, I pushed my frail mother on her cot and left the house at night. I was a school principal then. My mother, limping , looked for me in every corner with Tamosha. My anger extinguished when Ma was consigned to the flames on 11th June, 1998.

I remember once I got very late in reaching home, there was no telephone in our house or school. Mobile phones were yet to reach India. My mother was standing anxiously in the street with my brother, neighbour, my wife, and it was 1.30am and my father did not express his tension, he was lying in bed.

"Are you a butcher!" my mother reacted. My father complained about my mother, but to my utter surprise I saw that they both were cool and did not quarrel. My arrival at home safely delighted them. On one occasion my students went to meet my mother, she did not want to show her skeletal shape. I forced her to come out. She came and said: 'I am Jesus on the cross. Why do you want to meet my poor self?'

Ma was good at sports, played badminton, participated in dramas, and wore bobbed hair when she was in Rangoon. Once her father was late in coming home from office, it was almost 10pm. She ran to the Rangoon Secretariat Building, but security personnel did not allow her, so she climbed the boundary wall. World War II destroyed her dreams. After marriage, Mrs Decory, Ma's English teacher reprimanded my grandfather for marrying Ma off and not allowing her to study further, she was catapulted from Rangoon to a remote village of East Pakistan. Just a month before her death, the Government of India tested Nuclear Bombs on 11th May 1998. "Political leaders are shunning innumerable crises, they are after nuclear explosions. Rubbish! We should boycott them forever. How the misanthropists are running the government of the world," she asked.

She said this at a time when we were all ecstatic as India joined the super power club. She had no love for the warmonger governments of the world because of her sufferings in World War II. She revolted helplessly against some political jokers before she breathed her last. Ma was imaginative about her children, tolerated longstanding stress and strain for making us gems. I had been living in my wife's flat opposite to my parents. My eldest brother brought hiatus in our family. He had a new flat of his own and took off with his wife. My ailing mother was staying with my old short-tempered father and equally moody youngest brother. All three in a small flat and I was their poorest support. They failed to fathom my mother's catastrophe. I was foolish and my wife did not help me improve my mother's condition.

I got mentally aberrated regarding her health and tried to cover up my idiocy by paying money to her in installments every month. On 10th June 1998, I reached her with a meager amount to help her as usual. I could not hand it over to her. She was in a stupor. "Your mother stinks profusely," my father told me.

They did not allow me to employ an ayah for my mother and she could not bathe properly. She used to take sleeping pills intermittently to get rid of the excruciating pain in her stomach. After her cremation I was informed that she had cancer. Probably everyone in our family knew it much before and suppressed it from me lest I might go beyond my financial capacity for her treatment. "Everyone in the world must get the right to die in comfort," once Mother Teresa said when she was nursing a dying destitute from Calcutta's footpath.

We did not accord our most beloved one proper treatment for a single second. We all betrayed her and we lost the most precious person of our family. It was the first tragedy of our family. After cremation, when I returned, we experienced for the first time our house sans' mother.

"Your mother swallowed a good number of quinine after a bickering with me and you were in pre-natal stage in your mother's womb. She was vomiting intermittently. She thought she might beget a twin. And your mother was tremendously anxious for you always," said my father. Father was totally a different man from that day. He was calm, quiet, keen on getting my company, forlorn, sequestered. He stepped into my mother's shoes. My father died one year seven months later. He was then just the facsimile of my mother in behavior. He was a neglected man till he died. None of his children spent a single farthing for him apart from his *Shradh.*"

3

I am always afraid of death. At age seven, I held a mirror and got horrified seeing my own face. I threw it, and ran aimlessly. I did not get to see my real self in the reflected image. I felt the futility of my existence. I ran, ran, and ran and could not get rid of the feeling. Almost after ten minutes I was able to be free from that horrifying condition of my nothingness. I failed to eat, read and dress properly, I did not tell anyone about this bizarre feeling of mine. I was outrageously afraid of death and even today I am awfully frightened. I spoilt precious years feeling this eeriness and misunderstood by all. I disliked my existence, my whereabouts. Probably I was suffering temporary insanity. When I was in Class V, one wintry morning, the cobbler Holuda's ailing wife died. I saw her cremation, her physical body consigned into flames and the same odd feeling enveloped me.

Forty-three years ago, we migrated to India from erstwhile East Pakistan. Had I again become oblivious of a traumatic mind? My father's financial problem was a burning issue then. I was influenced by my uncle to be a monk of Ramakrishna mission. I was the most perfect boy when I first visited Dakshineshwar with my father. Life style in erstwhile East Pakistan and that of Calcutta was diametrically opposite. Field of my imagination and reverie expanded remarkably and I felt myself to be a disciple of Swami Vivekananda. I spent my time in great joy. Every moment was a spiritual moment to me.

In DNK Project, most of my father's bosses apart from the superintendent of education were worthless compared to him and he suffered under those incompetent people. He surprisingly conceded to the extreme odds of the project for the sake of his family, his children. He was transferred to Kapsi, a remote corner of DNK Project as a token of punishment. I had wide variety vicissitude there. Once Tarapada da, a helpless peon reached my father for he needed a few school students to cremate his wife. I was in a school interspersed with poor refugee children from Bangladesh. Me and *mejda* joined the team of volunteers for cremation. Seeing the dead body burning on the funeral pyre, my latent fear of death resurrected again. I reached home in the evening completely metamorphosed, shattered as I was years ago seeing the dead body of Holuda's wife at Batajore in Barisal. I began reading books on sex, with vulgar pictures of the worst type to forget that riddle of existence. Fear of death, evil spirits, isolation, apathy for life enveloped my whole existence.

Our school shifted to Pakhanjore, an urban town. In the rush of shifting and seeing many attractive girls in the new school made my apathy for life evanescent. I gradually turned normal, participated in dramas and was acclaimed several times. But I used to feel that I was born for a great work. Despite my frailties in studies, I felt in me an abnormally ambitious man during my school days, imagining I would never die, my father would never die. I was after girls for I believed that I would marry the most beautiful and highest educated lady of the world. One event was extremely disturbing to me.

The dullest period of my life was college days in Raipur. I was away from my parents, my turmoil was internal, I grew long hair and began wearing flair cut trousers. My *dada* sometimes sent money to me from Calcutta, not a large amount, but enough to maintain prevalent fashion. I managed to be a graduate somehow. My medium was English; lectures of History and Political Science were given in Hindi. Most books in these subjects were in Hindi. I tried to translate but I had no tutor. My aim in life reached the lowest nadir. I just wanted to be a smart medical representative.

Since I met Khuku di in 1972, my only aim was to stay in Calcutta and enjoy Bengali culture. Khuku di was a distant relative. She was pretty and sang well. I was greatly influenced with Satyajit Ray, Mrinal Sen, Uttam Kumar, Aparna Sen, Suchitra Sen, Lady Ranu, Samaresh Bose and many others. When I was a salesman in a shop on Rashbehari Avenue I saw many, including Suchitra Sen, I first heard of Sen from my mother, while she was chatting with my father's colleagues in a big kitchen room in the headmaster's quarters at Dhulia of Barisal.

Dhulia was at that time a big village interspersed with poor Hindus and well-off Muslims. My father's quarters were by a canal and the house was sprawling. There was a big meadow in front and it ended at the horizon. Aftaluddin Mian, a tall, fair learned and shrewd man, Sufi Mian, lean and thin and '*panchwaqt namazi admi*' and good soul, Ghiasuddin Sahib who looked like a

European and his wife, Mahiuddin, Sufi Mian's eldest son were our neighbours.

In 1959 we went to Calcutta for seven months. We returned to Dhulia nine months after for we stayed in the city of Barisal near Kaonia Crematorium. That was a marvelous experience. After our comeback, Dhulia became a romantic place for me. Its panoramic view was incredibly beautiful. The autumnal clouds in the azure sky, greenery, grazing cattle, rain tree, school and silent masjid over Headmaster's chamber, field in front of the school, jet black night in winter, hooting of owls, nocturnal silence, khajur trees, khajur's *ras*, mother's delicious dishes, clouded moonlit nights, summer time's palash flower, gave me astounding joy and a sense of fulfillment. My mind was partially urbanized due to my brief stay in Calcutta and the city of Barisal. My tastes changed. My father organized Saraswati Puja in school. Ninety percent of the students were Muslims. In spite of it the aura of the puja was unique. Alamgir, Mehboob, Alamda joined *arati* with Nandida, Ratneswarda, Brojenda.

The sequel was dangerous. Obstinate *maulavis* got chagrined with my father, they were members of the School Managing Committee. My father was a hard nut to crack. He used to read the holy Quran, the Geeta, and the Holy Bible. He had no abhorrence for any religion and sect. He was very popular with the students and guardians. Committee members failed to remove my obstinate father from Dhulia. Ultimately, they resorted to a partial dacoity. He had the salary of his staff in his big suitcase. The clerk of the school came when my father was putting it safely by his bed. That night he had the portal of his door open and was reading till midnight. He was preparing for MA examination in English. He fell asleep. Four goons entered through the open door, had his suitcase, his warm clothes and suits, his certificates of all kinds. The goons had rustic weapons. They bagged our *kansa* utensils along with molasses from the jar and a single denture of my mother kept in a glass of water. My mother saw them in the dim light of the lantern, by the wooden table, by my father's bed, and she got nervous and dumbfounded. She cried feebly, my father woke up. Instantly one of the miscreants hurled my father's lantern away, the chimney broke, the room was stark dark.

They ran out, my father chased them alone but those *goonda*s receded in the murky meadows. Villagers, mock sympathizers and good men poured into our house. It was almost 3.30am. The strategy chalked out by the scoundrels against my father was a grand success. Slowly the dejected morning arrived. My father went to school for official work. It was the month of holy Ramjan. The school was closed. We had no dishes to have our meals. Somehow my mother tried desperately to serve us meals. My father was awfully grave. He was groaning after having his meal late in the afternoon. The entire staff salary was in the stolen suitcase. My mother was consoling him, my father was in tears. All on a sudden my mother discovered that Mukti, my only sister was not in the house. Chandan, Shakti, my elder brothers and I jumped outside to find her out. *Dada* (Chandan) was just ten years old and *Mejda* (Shakti) was two years younger. Mother kept herself calm but her restlessness surfaced. My father got tremendously jittered and jumped into the pond and frantically searched for Mukti. Dipankar, my youngest brother was just two years old and could not understand anything. I was shrieking like a lunatic.

Meanwhile Dada ran to a boy, cordoned off by some sari clad little girls. The boy had dyed her face red with alta. He was in shorts which nearly fell to his toe, and the shirt was up to his knee, standing with close cropped hair, and bat-like eyes. We all ran to that boy because we recognized him to be Mukti, my only sister. She was tonsured as she had lice in her hair just a few months ago. She was taken to Daftarida's (my father's peon) house. His daughters decorated Mukti. Both her shirt and shorts belonged to *mejda.* My defeated father got angry, he jumped out of the pond, gave Mukti a tight slap. She cried furiously. I got delighted getting her back and stopped shrieking. Things became somewhat normal ultimately with Mukti Sunderi – the beauty queen.

Two days after my father was taking a siesta on a wooden cot when there was a knock at the door. It was Alam, an alumnus of Dhulia High School. He had a long conversation with my father till evening and we discovered hundreds of goondas at the behest of notorious Mohiuddin had gheraoed my father. Alam joined them and created furore against my father. Alam, months ago joined the *arati* in Saraswati Puja and he now joined the ghost dance with Mohiuddin, the scoundrel. It was now crystal clear who intrigued to get our house robbed off.

My father was puzzled for a short while but he was never nervous. He faced the mob, I experienced for the first time how it felt when someone dared to give my father nasty slangs. Had my father heard Mohiuddin the matter would have become dangerous, for my father would have been murdered. Mohiuddin's *chamchas* and hired goons were prepared to destroy a great personality in the rural world of erstwhile East Pakistan. My dream, imagination, love for Dhulia were slowly disappearing. We all were keen on leaving Dhulia forever. The second officer from Boufal police station Prabhat Rajan Debnath came along with his lieutenants. He was quite tall, handsome, bespectacled and had a gorgeous voice. He gradually became my father's friend. He regarded my mother as his own *Boudi* (sister-in-law). We left Dhulia forever. When our big boat started in the evening, *daftari dada* was crying forlornly sitting on the bank. Within a year *daftari dada* died, falling from a coconut tree in front of his own house.

4

We reached Kalisuri, a bit urbanized place where my *sejo jethamahasay* (third elder brother of my father) was a union board doctor. We shortly took off for Barisal and put up at Alekanda, a place for sophisticated people and got admitted to Adarsha Vidyapith in class one. My father got a temporary teacher's job in Sadar Girls School. He was very popular, he spoke King's English. Our life style and way of thinking became diametrically different. My mother used to attend prayer and rituals at Barisal Ramakrishna Mission. My father loved to go to Bholagiri Ashram. We began getting urbanized according to style of the city of Barisal. Dhulia's traumatic memory was lost.

I loved the Ramakrishna Mission the most. One fine morning a queer sound came from the sky, we all boys and urchins began running with the sound of the flying object. It was a small helicopter. It landed at Barisal police line. I was excited seeing European nuns bicycling through the main road and watched the handsome European fathers. I learnt swimming and was a good swimmer and hoped to get prizes but yet have not got any.

Barisal is famous for great men like Aswini Kumar Dutta, BM College, BM School, Zilla School, Satin Sen. Aswini Kumar (AK) Hall was named Ayub Khan Hall at the time of the reign of field Marshall Ayub Khan from Royal Military Academy of Sandhurst. He was a military dictator of unpartitioned Pakistan. General JN Choudhury, the chief of the army staff in the post Sino Indian combat era was a close friend of Ayub Khan in Sandhurst. When we left Barisal and our original homeland in 1964, he was still ruling.

I saw hordes of exquisitely beautiful girls. But none seemed to be a complete individual to me. One evening I was waiting for a bus at Panditiya wearing a clumsy dress and torn shoes. Suddenly I felt that I was a historical giant trudging through an undulating path. I had many sleepless nights and dreamt of becoming the husband of the most beautiful lady of the world. I was probably the worst selfish thinker without ideology. I discovered decades later in me, a lover, a believer of world unification, a total hater of war, arms and weapon race. Thirty years after I came to know that Greta used to haunt the departmental stores of our vicinity when I was a counter salesman. Her only companion was her mother. During Durga Puja in 1975 she was hobnobbing in the puja pandal of Triangular Park. Even I was there for hours. Just a few years before during my stay at Raipur, I wanted to be a medical representative in Calcutta and now I am ambitious to be the greatest lover!

I managed to be a Post Graduate from the Ravi Shankar University as an external candidate from that sales counter. After my return from Raipur after finishing my MA Final Examination I was not re employed by Prabirda, later he re-employed me in 'Craze' as a counter salesman. I was working in 'Craze' in the second phase almost for one year.

After Tamosha's mother died, Tamosha boarded the train to return. They came back shattered, fatigued, weather beaten. I reached in that morning but she did not talk to me. I was waiting, offered help of any sort, she refused. On my way back home the next evening I went to her house again with fruits. She was in her small bedroom with Pratim Dasgupta, her senior office colleague. Tamosha went to the gate to see him off and came back fifteen minutes later. I got more involved with her. Pratim's wife was staying in Canada and he was on the verge of taking off from India. Five days later on a Sunday evening, I came again to meet her and she was busy talking to Akash, her ex-fiance. Akash was tall, handsome, girlish and swaggering. His approach was better than Pratim. I got myself affianced with Tamosha. Knowing full well that she did not love me and she also had no choice. My relation with her improved till Bappa, a new recruit joined her office. Their warm relations made her desperate and ruthless about me.

My mother left for Bhopal for my sister's house. I had no respite to express my sorrow, developed insomnia and began smoking. I was teaching Tamosha spoken English, yoga and ways of grooming herself. She became inattentive. One day I lost my cool and slapped her. She told me to go back to my mother to improve my mental disorder. I came to know two decades after that my Greta was not married then but I did not know Greta at that time. And I married Tamosha after my mother's comeback. But her relation with Bappa and Akash continues till this date. Pratim had gone to Canada. One and a half years after I fathered a beautiful baby boy. Only he prevented us from separation.

In my son's childhood Tamosha made her bed separate. My mother was suffering from asthma, lung bleeding, spondylitis. My father came back from Dandakaranya permanently. I was separated from the family by my elder brother and his wife. I took shelter in Tamosha's flat. Within a year our elder brother left my parents and youngest brother, for, he owned a flat of his own. I did not break down completely for all the difficulties that I had to face but it was extremely tiring. I continued to be engaged in more private tuitions to run both the families. My father had a meagre pension, my youngest brother earned but it was not at all sufficient.

At school I established 'World Unification League' to run a massive movement. We received no salary for nine months. I was full of enthusiasm to control the bridle of the world instead of controlling the bridle of all my problems hanging around me. Tamosha was a central government employee but contributed nothing. She squandered whimsically. She gave me shirts, shoes, socks, trousers whenever she liked. I ran from one place to another to earn more. I was still the most ambitious man of the world.

Chapter 10
Idea of World Unification

1

The chairman of the school's managing committee sometimes stayed at Puri. I was sent with Gobind Choudhury, another teacher to bring him back. It was 1985, I was beaten up by two pandas of the Puri Jagannath temple as they coerced for money and I protested. Since then, I have a bad neck despite a major operation. But my second visit brought joy. I reached the temple with Gobind and could feel Chaitanya Mahaprabhu everywhere. On my way back I befriended two beautiful British girls who were tourists. I shall never forget them, particularly the one who stroked my hair when I was sleeping in the bunk at night.

I returned to Howrah next morning. In the evening a meeting of the Managing Committee was scheduled. Our lady Principal resigned and handed over the charge to me. I was made acting Principal. Many of my colleagues agitated but they could not bring about any change. One hostile group of teachers went to the Head Office in Delhi, headed to meet Mr. Cotton. I too went to Delhi to meet him. Mr. Cotton gave me audience and my small team was with me. I was verbally abused by him and left his office. He served me a notice cancelling our school's affiliation. We then went to the High Court against this notice and the good judge gave stay order. In the aftermath of this drama Gobind, Alpana and Srikumar, my so-called friends leveled a charge of embezzlement against me. Audit works of school accounts was not done by the MC for eight consecutive years. Very many lapses were exhumed by the auditor. Subsequently many important financial documents and papers were stolen by Gobind, Alpana and Srikumar in connivance with the chairman. All these hassles were overcome by active and psychological guidance of some of my generous colleagues and MC members.

Meanwhile, the world around us was changing too. Before I became acting Principal, Rajiv Gandhi was killed brutally.

Nazibulla of Afghanistan was hanged, USSR collapsed after introduction of fictitious Glasnast and Prestorika by Gorbachev. Boris Yeltsin started running the government. 'Duma' relaunched. Nelson Mandela was released after prolonged incarceration for 27 years. Bill Clinton defeated George Bush senior. Innumerable innocent civilians in Iraq were killed by Bush Junior's war monger policy. Terrorists' wrath competed with natural calamity like tsunami and global warming. Some of the Gulf countries like Afghanistan and Pakistan started patronizing global terrorism. In India regime of coalition government had its breakthrough after Narasimha Rao.

Indo-American nuclear deal kept hanging in the balance, for Left Front's conventional policy. Myanmar was burning and Aung San Suu Kyi was in incarceration. Sir Vidiadhar Surajprasad Naipaul received Nobel Prize in literature. In 'Picador India' his assessment of Gandhi is unique. He wrote, "Was it dhoti, the spinning wheel, the homespun, the Thoreau, the Ruskin, the sexual abstinence, the vegetarianism, the Christian hymns, the refusal to drink cow's milk, the latrine cleaning? It was impossible for anyone to be a complete Gandhian; no one could make that pioneer journey again; people had to take the one or two things they liked from the menu. In the main they took the homespun; that was the easiest and most stylish item." Sir VSN furthermore wrote on Mahatma, "The saintly half-clad figure Aldous Huxley saw on the rostrum in Kanpur in 1925 was not wholly Indian, as Huxley thought. The best part of Gandhi in 1925 had really been London and South Africa."

No writing, no book, no lecture, no film, no great man could fathom Gandhi to that impeccable range. Opinion of Naipaul on Vinoba Bhave is dangerously westernized. In 1977 my maternal uncle came from London for 21 days. "Is Vinoba Bhave still alive?" he asked with sarcasm. He expressed opinion on Loknayak Jayprakash with identical sarcasm. Identically Sir Naipaul stated, "There was a foolish man, Vinoba Bhave…" He browsed India, its heritage through a westerner's eye. Naipaul furthermore stated, "Indian writers to speak generally seem to know only about their own families and their places of work." Does it really hamper readers' pleasure? Charles Dickens was far more astounding and phenomenal writer than Naipaul. He even appreciated with cynical tinge. He criticizes Nirad C Chowdhury scrupulously but he resembles Chowdhury at least in geocentricism. Both were on foreign land and self-centered cynics. Mahatma was pristinely assessed, measured and described only by the brilliant people of the west. Romain Rolland, Louis Fisher, David Lean, Richard Attenborough are among those outstanding brilliant minds. He was adored by King Martin Luther (Jr.), Nelson Mandela and Barrack Obama. He was partially deified by Einstein. Charlie, you also met him in London slum and was all praise for him.

Greta and Henrietta were not at all conscious of this matter. They were not intellectually inclined. They loved glamour, beauty, power, own administrations, families, children, mothers and husbands. Tamosha was flaunting family norms flamboyantly against my will. I was traumatized, handicapped by her negligence. Bappa Ganguly was the only photographer in our wedding ceremony and at our reception both Bappa and Tamosha were exchanging fond looks. Six months after our marriage we went to see a movie 'Sphinx.' Uma my colleague, her sister, myself, Tamosha, Bappa and his friend sat in a row. Bappa happened to sit by me. Tamosha desperately tried to go out. I asked Bappa to sit beside her and Bappa sat. Tamosha's anger melted. Bappa turned a frequent visitor to our house. I could not settle down, to do a B. Ed. and tried to get myself engaged in extra work returning home late at night. I deliberately made myself tired, so that I shall not get chance to poke my nose in Tamosha's affairs. Every day was a nightmare to me. I began loving spiritual causes and read voraciously. Gradually I became oblivious of my ignoble failure in loving Tamosha. It was so excruciatingly painful that I imagined my death very often.

2

One morning I was preparing question papers for weekly test in my mother's house on the ground floor and Bappa reached. Tamosha was helping me, her sister called from her first floor house, "Hi *Didi*, Bappa da has come." Tamosha jumped off to meet him immediately. I entreated her to stay for a short while, she did not listen. My son was just three years old. In the afternoon he began crying for his mother, it was summer and I got ready in that sweltering heat, took him with me, a bag for my tuition and reached his mother's office. I was sandwiched with my son in the crowded bus. I had no fund for hiring a cab. I got down at Park Street, put my son on my shoulder and walked up to Wood Street and reached his mother's office perspiring. I asked the security personnel, he told, *"O to jahan tak mera khayal hai Bappa sahib ke saath kahin ghoomne giya hai* (So far I know , she has gone somewhere with Bappa sahib). I put my son on my shoulder again and managed to return home. Love between Tamosha and Bappa was perfect, immaculate, wild, and it destroyed me. I did not want to believe it was happening, I loved her very much.

Gradually I became oblivious of defeat of my love. I was craving for a second child. I thought perhaps it would solve all problems between Tamosha and me. She conceived thereafter and got it aborted. Nine years after she agreed to mother another child but by then she lost her capacity to conceive. My dream to father a second child was thus lost. Meanwhile, Dorothy Chatterjee joined as a part time teacher, a short, petite woman. She was a born genius, an extraordinary singer, an extrovert, had a legacy of talent from her father who was already dead. She loved my eyes while I loved her talent and looks. I had a stormy love relation with her for six months. She was the only unmarried girl I ever fell for. Her father had a good library and she did not read a single book. She expressed her wish to elope with me, which I disliked. By twenty-seven she happened to mix with a good number of senior male friends. Dorothy could not tolerate my only son and flayed Tamosha nakedly. She was my son's private tutor. One evening when I reached her house my son was all alone. Dorothy was busy practising song in an adjacent room. I went to their library on the mezzanine floor. Dorothy asked my son to go back home. He did not know about my presence. He was in light blue jeans and red T shirt. He was slowly walking to the main road, I discovered a ruthless father in me and I completely removed Dorothy from my life forever.

My well cherished idea of 'World Unification League' dried away. I had to tackle hordes of litigations in school. We need a society where lovers will never be jinxed. I felt Egalitarianism would be banished throughout the globe for upsurge of market economy. We cannot deny Marx the philosopher though the so-called communist juggernauts have thrown him into hurly burly.

Mahatma and Mother Teresa are astounding characters. Mahatma Gandhi was well understood and followed to a great extent by King Martin Luther (Jr.), Nelson Mandela and Nino Aquino. Non-violence and love for mankind without any censored religious message was preached only by Gandhi in this planet. Its vibration is becoming omnipresent and omnipotent. Dr APJ Abdul Kalam, our former President and phenomenal scientist expressed hope to see a new world in his speech at the Rice University, Houston USA. He said on October 20, 2007: "....ignite the minds" of students to inspire them to make discoveries. Dr APJ Abdul Kalam proposed establishing a 'World Space Council' which could oversee the planning and implementation of "exploration, space security and social missions."

Such unified approach will enable the world to see a quantum jump in the progress in space science and technology for the benefit of all the nations of the world. He anticipates that more international partnerships will be formed to help countries and organizations to share competencies and undertake the financial and management burdens associated with large, complex activities. Above the world space council proposed by him, he said "It could be with global participation to oversee the planning and implementation of exploration, space security and societal missions." Dr Kalam believed that with the advances in Science and Technology and future possibilities, what will be space profile in 2050, being provided with leadership by World Space Council.

They dreamt of a world where all citizens will have safe drinking water and use solar power. It would be a clean planet. By 2050, Dr Kalam believed, planet earth will be transformed to posterity without poverty, peaceful without fear of water and a happy place to live for the whole humanity using space technologies as one of the prime movers. Great men propose and bad men dispose, great men dream and bad men turn every dream into a nightmare, great men plan and evil men destroy, great men give philosophy and the evil exploit. Dr APJ being a scientist and philosopher might not think about the world of politicians and their diabolic muscles, though he was the first scientist in Rashtrapati Bhawan for five years. By 2050, the entire world civilization can live in tremendous prosperity in accordance with Dr APJ Kalam, if only politicians stop pouring from the bottom benches of the world.

In the modern world none reached out the Upanishads like Tagore. His goal was to utilize it in man for man and for our best development. He wrote "It is men of world mind that we need, men of the spirit, that we need to see that we are citizens of the kingdom of ideas… there will be men large enough to see the human race as a whole, who understand that the good of humanity as a family actually exists." He launched an educational crusade in his *ashram.* He dreamt to establish an international university with best mindset of all races. It would mingle and interact and would create a mammoth global human race. Had his philosophy been accepted by the world we would have got a shining world society. He had reservation on Gandhian boycott lest it might hurt the poor. He expressed it in his famous novel '*Ghare Baire*'. But it did not mar his relation with Gandhi. Mutual respect was there between two all-time greats. After the World War I, Tagore's *Gitanjali* was read in the houses of the West. Phenomenal film director David Lean of Hollywood was influenced by '*Gitanjali*' in his youth after that ignoble first Great War. It is learnt that he was popularly accepted by the West. His books were easily available in the book-stalls of England and America. But today we seldom get his works in those countries. He was an outstanding humanist. After Jallianwala Massacre in 1919 he refused British Knighthood and probably the pundits and politicians of the West reacted and relinquished Tagore. Great poet T S Eliot once said, "Tagore is not my cup of tea." Poets like Emerson, Ezra Pound and his onetime friend W B Yeats developed antipathy for him. The world failed to understand him and his greatness. At the same time clerics of Santiniketan made Tagore their God but failed miserably to follow his doctrines.

3

Meanwhile, Calcutta Film Festival was boycotted by Aparna Sen, Rituparna and many others for Nandigram Tragedy. Just two days ago, our school got over much earlier than usual. Some hired goons attacked our students in front of our school and began thrashing some boys randomly. Hearing it I ran outside to stop. One of them hurled a blow on the upper corner of my right eye, it bled and my spectacles broke, I fell down. Our students got furious, caught hold of the hooligans, three ran away. I was taken to a local hospital for treatment. Four goons were taken to police custody. After my comeback from the hospital, I called a staff council's meeting. The goons were sure that I would sue them in the criminal court, but I informed the police station all about it and those four young miscreants of a political party were released at 10.30pm. Every country of our civilized planet is like this or worse than this.

I believe our posterity shall get the world united someday, my father inculcated this belief in me. I discussed twenty-five years ago with Mr. S P Banerjee, ex-teacher of Hindi High School, a highly dignified man who stood first in LLB from Benares Hindu University. He was the home tutor of a Prince in Rajasthan before 1947. "I believe in one world government, though I will not be able to see but you must try to inculcate in your students values like how to save fauna and flora, how to save nature."

His grandchild Aditya was my private student and at present he is in Sweden. I developed interest in learning quotations from the Upanishads and the Gita from SP Banerjee. He was one of the most outstanding optimists even at seventy-nine. He was elder than my father by ten years but used to address me 'Sir' when I was hardly twenty-eight. He was my one of the greatest teachers.

"Every country, every state even every village and hamlet of the world shall not lose its own identity in the world government in real sense of the term. We should assassinate violence without bloodshed. Migratory birds are killed in Afghanistan for rich dishes. Sparrow to eagle shall live like hand in gloves. Flowers shall get sweeter smell, bees will create better honeycombs," Mr. Banerjee said to me in a strange fit of passion. He quoted from King Author of Tennyson,

> "The old order changeth, yielding place to new,
> And God fulfils himself in many ways,
> Lest one good custom should corrupt the world.

But see what we have done finally! What a fiasco! Nandigram burnt, Calcutta burnt due to Taslima Nasreen's book, intellectuals, artists, actors, theatrical ombudsmen protested, in Assam *adivasis* were tortured, bombs were blasted in Benares, Lucknow and Faizabad. If Taslima really hurts the religious sentiments of any community it's painful and ignoble in all respects. But is '*fatawa*' a solution? One should get chance for rectification. In 'Meghnadbadh Kavya' Michael Madhusudan Dutta dwarfed Lord Rama very many times. Was Michael ostracized or hanged? Fundamentalism is increasing by leaps and bounds. It might gradually take a diabolic shape of worst order. Fanatics and chauvinists are more powerful than philanthropists and good men these days. I ran amuck to Greta several times to ask her to resort to an effort to work out solution and she asked me to write. I told her, "Were Buddha and Jesus writers? They popularized maximum peace and love for mankind, love for animals. Greta, you can't expect anybody to pacify this ferocious world by writing only. Terrorists and mafias are running parallel governments and banditry of all sorts cannot be changed unless majority of the world masses are not united and courageous."

This is a failure on the part of civilization.

Meanwhile, Greta was supposed to go to Delhi to meet Harjeet. I called her up, she asked me to meet her.

"I rang up Harjeet, he wants to meet you in Calcutta shortly," she said.

"He will kill me," I replied.

"You forgot you are the founder of the 'World Unification League'. You wanted to unify the world into a single super state. Why will you while away your valuable time after me? I can't be a subject of your research. Do research with the world and mankind and man's future," she told.

"My prolonged struggle compelled to tolerate every oddity in you." I did not lose my temper.

I love mankind. I love the world, I love the world unification. Leaving everything aside I began developing the concept of love incessantly. The world is my home, I consider myself a global citizen. Every living being, fauna and flora is my family. I love the blue sky, dry desert, snow peaked mountains, beauty of girls and boys, of men and women. When I see anyone in rags, I get bewildered. Why should I while away my whole time after Greta? While I thought about the world, its welfare, its grandeur; she probably thought about Harjeet.

"We got transferred from Jalandhar to Kashmir," she finally came up with the truth. "I could not pack off our luggage. I had a tremendous trauma. We were together for more than a year. I went to his village, stayed there for three nights." Whenever we talked, Harjeet was the most important topic of conversation.

I replied: "Greta, I will no longer exhaust my 'valuable time' on friends like you. I have got to make a journey to unify man, to free the world from terrorism, religious fanaticism. There are millions like me in the world and each individual is equally precious. Only our conglomeration may bring a new dimension, a new tinge, a new enthusiasm."

"Don't be that proud. Your pride doesn't allow you to be a real lover. At this age you should get no choice but to stay with me, with your family and the school. No imagination. Unification of the world is a process in evolution, no man can expedite this process," she returned.

"World of man always needs leaders. That's why we got George Washington, Lincoln, Gandhi, Sun Yat-sen, and Mandela. Process of progress of man is always expedited by great leaders. How dare you ignore them?" I retorted.

"I don't ignore. But will you be able to reach their level in your life time? Morning shows the day. Don't over estimate yourself," she returned.

"Don't underestimate me," I told.

"Who the hell am I to estimate your good self-Sir? What programme have you chalked out for braving this invincible project? You are simply an emotional fool. Great leaders are born, they never did great work as an optional subject," she returned.

"World unification was always my first choice, it is still my first choice and I founded 'World Unification League' with that objective," I said.

"It's an immature work of a young teacher, it was more of a fiasco," she returned.

I asked, "Greta! Will you go now? It's a Sunday."

We went out. We did not have a car, so we walked. It was April, scorching heat was burning us. I was sweating and so was she. We took a cab. I dropped her off. Coming back home I lay on the sofa and fell asleep. I woke in the evening and began contemplating; will my God of Unification of the World really die unwept and unsung? Shall I not be able to bring about any change in the world? Am I really incompetent? I failed to fathom the sea of thought. Tamosha stopped talking to me. Even my son avoided me. Yet we lived in a single house under one roof.

Probably I told you Charlie, Tamosha was a government official. I loved her, and I loved Greta. But my love for man was vastly superior. Chaitanya Mahaprabhu lost his first wife whom he loved dearly and married again. But he could not settle his mind in family life. His love for his first wife was ultimately converted into love for Man, love for Krishna. He sacrificed everything and became a sannyasi.

4

I wrote a letter to Mr. Walker A Diamanti, the ex-Consul General of American Consulate, Calcutta to seek his guidance for World Unification League, but did not receive any response. I wrote to Nelson Mandela, Bishop Desmond Tutu, Bill Clinton and they did not respond. I did not lose enthusiasm. I am always optimistic, I dreamt to conquer the world with love. For more than three months I had no connection with Greta. I spent sleepless nights remembering my late parents. One night I lay fast asleep and had a peculiar dream, it resuscitated my drowning hope.

In my dream I reached an occidental city to attend an International Conference on World Unification. It was a special hall and it was a round table conference. Einstein, Gandhi, Tolstoy, Kennedy, Martin Luther King (Jr.), Nelson Mandela, Bill Gates, Dalai Lama were sitting together. I sat with Greta and with very many personages not known to me. JFK started some of his oration rendered by me, "Every idiot can start a war. Let us pray…. that there will be no veterans of any further war – because all shall have learned to live together in peace. We face a relentless struggle in every corner of the globe. I claim not to have controlled events, but confess plainly that events have controlled me. There is no cause half as sacred as the cause of the people. There is no idea as uplifting as the idea of service to humanity. We are not boasters and buffoons of the terror of life, and we must mean ourselves to face it. I dream things that never were – and I say: Why not?........" I was mesmerised by the astounding and phenomenal beginning of the speech of

President Kennedy, Martin Luther King (Jr.) clapped first and all followed him. Greta stood up gave my introduction they all clapped again. I was told to express my views but did not dare open my lips. I was keen on listening to Martin Luther King (Jr.) and Bill Gate. I did not want to deliver a speech of my own. I heard a voice from All India Radio. It was in Hindi. It was the voice of Gandhi. My sleep broke. Our pet, Cassius was barking.

The school was closed for summer vacation. We started a massive renovation of our school. For that massive construction we decided to reopen the school a bit late on 3rd July instead of 26 June. It was my only son's birthday. But all the teachers were asked to attend. Greta came as a rule, went back home earlier without asking me. In the afternoon she left her home and went out. She told me she was going for shopping with her mother and grandmother. I did not know her grandmother. None in her family knew where she went. At midnight, I telephoned and she disconnected. I could fathom something fishy. Greta told me several times before, "I broke my relation with Harjeet for you." I realised she loved Harjeet more than she loved me.

Next morning, I met Greta and was keen to express my feelings. "Greta, I did not want to drag my monotonous life, I want to be free from bondage, from clutches of my family, friends and you too. I failed to keep pace into the world of my imagination. I am pained to see fighting, killings, massacre, poverty, corruption, bigotry. I want to put an end to political 'dhandabaji', notorious politicians, parallel underground governments, Mafia Raj worldwide, and want to love you till I die." She did not reply.

Meanwhile I went to Bangalore with my family, friends and officials to attend a seminar of Independent Schools' Federation. The seminar continued for three days. We stayed for two more days and during that span Bush killed Saddam. "Saddam, Saddam, Saddam" barked Bush for more than half a decade. Identically his ancestors killed Salvador Allende, Patrice Lumumba, Che Guevara and many other political giants of the world. At present global warming is a bigger danger than global terrorism. Antarctic, Arctic and all ice covers of this planet are melting. Trees are felled mercilessly, business tycoons or general public pay no attention. Mere teaching of 'Environmental Education' in class rooms of schools will bring no remarkable change. It shall fail as teaching of 'Moral Science' failed.

Chapter 11
Thrown into Prison

1

I was tired of fighting with myself. I have decided to shift from writing letters to you Charlie and instead write to my students. Today every inhabitant of this planet must contemplate the way when it may no longer be habitable. Every man, woman and child is under a nuclear sword of Damocles, hanging by the slenderest of threads capable of being cut at any moment by accident, miscalculation or madness. The weapons of war must be abolished before they abolish us. Many thinkers and philosophers made poverty their mainstay and their books have vanquished the libraries, but why cannot be there a fructiferous result. The world was always without a leader of global stature and today things are worse.

I always enjoyed reading 'War and Peace' of Tolstoy. I had the book in my almirah also. I enjoyed a movie on this epical volume. Tolstoy left an indelible impression in my mind. In my boyhood during my stay in Bastar, I read about him in Hindi. His volcanic talent was dormant for a long time. Since he fled the Russian army he awoke, authored 'Resurrection', 'War and Peace', 'Anna Karenina' and many short stories. He made himself an apostle of peace and ombudsman for mankind, civilization and global progress of morality. Gandhi was impacted much by Tolstoy, Thoreau and Emerson during his movements in South Africa. I get disgusted when people criticize Gandhi without knowing Gandhi the man and Gandhi the Mahatma.

Erstwhile USSR's Gorbachev in reality took the first steps to advancement of human race. He is one of the most successful persons beyond controversy in the last century but resigned presidency in 1991 and is forgotten. He was the Prometheus of the world of today. According to Greek mythology Zeus wanted to keep man in primitivity but Prometheus belonged to the Titans, a race of the world before arrival of gods, stole fire from god and handed over to man, and man's progress began. Mikhail

Gorbachev was punished by the Russians and by all of us. The Soviet Russia collapsed in front of Gorbachev.

I remember in 1969 when I was at Pakhanjore. My father was the headmaster of Pakhanjore High School. It was the year of Gandhi centenary and my father monitored a wide variety of programmes and social projects with students. I was in Class X then. In the meantime, my paternal grandmother died in Barisal. My father was traumatized but led every other work like a colossus. Whereas all the third-class bureaucrats of Dandakaranya Refugee Project had a callous function. None came to our school despite my father's efforts amidst his misery. On the last evening of Gandhi Centenary Programme, in his oration, he compared Gandhi with Chaitanya Mahaprabhu and Tolstoy.

The world today is in a great jeopardy. It was never like this before. Stephen Hawking, the great astrophysicist has been locked in his body for motor neuron disease for many decades but does not only dream with the world but he dreams of man's empire in space. He even experienced zero gravity during flight over the Atlantic Ocean. He shall shortly embark upon an odyssey in the space. On one hand great men desire to give the world and this civilization an impetus and on the other hand, political vandals are rending the world for their caprice and whims.

Shall I be able to save my planet from inevitable collapse? Shall I be able to make my Mother Earth loved by her children? Democracy is a boon for us. But democracy is now giving birth to politicians who are crumbling our civilization, our planet, by incompetent and improper handling. In our supremely beautiful earth Lincoln, Gandhi, King Martin Luther (Jr.), Kennedy, Benigno Aquino Jr were murdered. Mandela was in incarceration for twenty-seven years. Novel and ultra-modern weapons are discovered every day for genocide, militarism, and militants are gaining currency. Fanatics from all sects are playing with man's life like mad. We go astray seeing movies creating war monger generations. Ignoble incidents of Virginia, Gurgaon, Louisiana allowed us to feel how insecure we are. Buddha, Jesus are only worshipped in temples. Priest craft is black mailing people. Romanticism is over ruled by unwritten regulations, though we all enjoy books with romantic affairs and films with romanticism. Innumerable people are dying helplessly from deadly diseases. AIDS has become an integral part of modern civilization. Yet death penalty of any sort by any authority is a severe crime. It's also a kind of murder. Dante, Virgil, Montesquieu, Rousseau, Hegel thought for man, wrote for men, and incompetent politicians of our age misuse it for their own benefits. Neither they read nor do they try to understand any philosophy.

Internet has made the world a global village, but negative social system is not allowing us to be in a single global family. Let us think about it seriously. Why we are not united? Why are we over ruled by the bigots in every age and every sphere! Ask your own conscience, your own God, to guide you. Your conscience is your greatest teacher. Gun powder culture culminated into the worst massacre in Hiroshima and Nagasaki. Violence gives rise to violence. Why are we not afraid of Nature's retaliation! Tsunami, earthquakes, natural cataclysms at least allowed us to believe its omnipotence. Why don't we love our docile but supremely powerful and exquisitely beautiful nature! But our beautiful nature can also turn dangerous. Even dinosaurs and billions of gigantic animals became extinct. How can humans think they will survive forever? Love Nature; take care of it as you take care of your dearest ones.

There is no pride in ruling the entire globe. The world itself has come from the universe. The longing for life created our planets and the same has created every life. It's very unfortunate that Mother Earth has a larger group of ruthless men to rule than prophets to save. Jesus was crucified, Socrates drank hemlock. The same ruthless ambience or far worse is still prevalent. Every man is an ambassador of the universe. Why should we believe that most of us are helpless? All the flabbergasted fools overpowered us for epochs together. Whereas sixty five percent penguins in the South Pole became extinct due to global warming. Alert! Alert! And be alert! I am begging for the awakening of your dormant consciousness. Don't go for applause and awards. Most prize givers are average men. Buddha, Jesus, Lincoln, Gandhi cared little for prizes. Make yourselves the best prizes to Mother Earth, to mankind.

Mother Earth needs you, mankind needs you. The universe and longing for life created the Sun and created us, created you, created me. We haven't come for destruction. Why shall we be casual when destruction of every sort is tangible?

"Every poor body is a temple of living God," according to Victor Hugo. Don't you see the blue sky? Don't you see the naked beggars? Don't you smell the rotten dead bodies lying on the battle fields? Do you believe Buddha really smiled at Pokhran? Our Sakyamuni was hurled the worst insult in that lunacy. Sophisticated goons are running most of the powerful political states and they utilize great names of great men for their own business. Patriotism is a virtue but far bigger boon is lying in unification of nations, unification of mankind. Why we are not united from the dawn of civilization! Western world has led the entire world to real modernization by its astounding and phenomenal scientific discovery. Our country began hibernating since the medieval period and went into the clutches of Europeans. After national liberation we began keeping pace with them. We are oblivious of our pride. Buddha, Jesus, Zarathustra, Prophet Mahomet are the greatest world contributors. We are gradually reaching the post-modern era without compatible mindset. We could not improve our mindset as science improved. Consequently, unique inventions are mishandled and shove us towards doomsday.

Billions are still living below poverty line in our planet. Stupendous expenditure in weapon's race by the name of national safety and security is luxury of worst order. If there be a third great war, it shall be a nuclear war, but the fourth one will be fought with hammer and chisel. War has to be treated as genocide. Omnipresent terrorism is the offspring of madding wars. Danger is coming from three dimensions. Terrorism, war between states and retaliation of Nature. T. S. Eliot expressed his agony in his phenomenal poem 'The Waste Land.' Our good earth is being used as wastepaper basket particularly by powerful lunatics. Alfred Nobel discovered dynamite but he had frustration for diabolical dynamism of dynamite. The Nobel Prize is the greatest recognition of quality in man. But some of the Nobel Peace prizes were given away to political bandits. Nobel Award Committee would have been honoured more if they had accorded peace laurel to Gandhi. The process of searching talents should be post modernized. That was why Jean Paul Sartre and Le Duc Tho of Vietnam refused Nobel Prize.

After Buddha, one of the greatest boons to us by omnipotent nature is Sri Ramakrishna. This flabbergasted world needs his message. We even failed to preach his message to the world.

Gandhi sometimes seemed to be an embodiment of Ramakrishna's message. But no greater message could influence the warmongers. After Sri Ramakrishna's demise, the World Wars ransacked the world and a culture of diasporas had its breakthrough. He breathed his last in 1886 and the World War I started in 1914. Chicago's religious conference could not impact the bloodsucking jackals. Benazir Bhutto was murdered by those blood sucking jackals. She was struggling to restore democracy in Pakistan. She was deliberately given no security by the dictatorial government. Very identically Rajiv Gandhi was given no proper deployment of security and was killed.

The entire world has become a bazaar and we have no choice. We demand innumerable achievements from our children and never let them enjoy their childhood. Our children are not racing horses. The industry will spoil your youth, your middle age shall be scuttled by disease and you will spoil your entire dream and talents by telling stories of your material achievements to your peers, children, and grandchildren. Competent students are thus hijacked and incompetent ones either go for secured job in government office or join politics. Exceptional cases are definitely there and with those exceptions our world is still running. Be bold and competent. Never fail to dream. Enjoy your creativity; enjoy the vibrant life around you. In our globe parallel underworld governments are in no way less powerful than the government who rule. Till date no concerted effort has been taken to cleanse this Augean stable. Dynamite lord, Alfred Nobel like Albert Einstein strongly opposed the military uses of his invention. Alfred Nobel gave a statement three years before his death – "For my part, I wish all guns with their belongings and everything could be sent to hell, which is the proper place for their exhibition and use."

Let's all start the movement here and now. Let the year be the 'International Year of the Mother Planet Earth.' Some international philanthropic organizations are also run by selfish, visionless, incompetent rich men. Don't depend on them. Come out from the scabbards, go ahead, be helmsmen, conquer the world with the best weapon ie. LOVE. If in our global family one portion of humanity is non-violent and peace loving, and maximum powerful people and organizations are violent, chauvinistic and fanatic, then the latter shall always win. The revolutions you are going to launch shall have to be scientific and rational. For the sake of the Mother Earth, its environment, its safety and security, and its longevity you shall have to be as serious as the terrorists are for their idiotic causes.

Most peace-loving people are extremely casual. As a result, all parochial systems and organizations are thriving. Our posterity will ridicule us for our unintelligent race even before the dawn of civilization. A single Lincoln or a single Gandhi shall always be killed. There has to be hordes of Lincolns, Gandhis, King Martin Luther (Jr.) amongst you. Strike the last nail on the coffin of violence, lethal weapons, chauvinism, fanaticism and bigotry. Failing which this planet shall shortly be a burning planet around the sun. Till this date the world is hecatomb for the whims and caprices of the heavyweight muscleman of our madding civilization. I am afraid how they will destroy Man, when you will destroy weapons and other machinery during that coveted revolution for unification. I am afraid; you are misguided by the entertainment media. Prognosis about the very many holy books is dangerous. Perpetual hope is prevalent in 'The Upanishads'. Tagore's life was an embodiment of the Upanishad. But nowadays his Santiniketan has also become a killing field. In every house, from the biggest place to the smallest hovel preach Tagore's dream, Ramakrishna's love, Gandhi's truthfulness, Kahlil Gibran's Internationalism. Mere celibacy shall crumble you. Sing song of John Lennon with all the students of the world, "Imagine there is no country…." Bid farewell to arms forever. Make our excellent village, Earth, an excellent place to live in. Search out the latent historical giants and colossuses who made mankind move with time.

I could not finish the letter that I started writing for my students. It was 1.35am. The school's durwans and security personnels were waiting for me. I left my chamber with all the letter pads, put it in a bag, bid them goodbye, hired a cab and reached Howrah Station. It was 2.30 am approximately. I ran across the platform. The train was moving out of the station to its destination. I didn't know where the train was actually going. And I had no ticket, I just boarded a moving train, sat in a vacant seat, and opened my bag, traced out the letter I was writing, browsed upon and began writing again. Probably I thought to send the letter by post. I felt relaxed as I was prepared with my heart and soul to face any eventuality.

I kept writing as the train chugged along to an unknown destination. I was almost in a trance, not knowing what I was doing, as if gripped by the energy of the cosmos.

I wrote to my students.

Children,

Nostradamus, the prophet gave predictions that were a source of inspiration to me. But I defy vehemently some of his superfluous predictions. His interpretations highlighted Napoleon and Hitler as anti-Christ. Napoleon belonged to a Christian family of Corsica; though in his coronation he denied the Pope but not Christianity. Hitler was born of a Christian mother and killed millions of Jews. Rather he was anti-Zionist. Both cannot be anti-Christ. Nostradamus made a forecast, "The Third World War will start from 2008 and the world will be destroyed." But I do not believe that the world can ever be destroyed by the whims and caprices of groups of fanatic and impotent so-called leaders. I never fancy denying my God 'Nature', my God 'Time', my God 'my Soul.' Let me die right on time and so should everybody. Did Nostradamus love the world!! Certainly not. I believe journey of man from the Universe and from Nothingness has a powerful significance. How omnipotence of TIME and NATURE shall be destroyed!

Think of Osama Bin Laden, the fanatic terrorist. He represents no community of the world in reality and is against civilization. In no way he can be given the logo of 'Anti-Christ.' He is just a madman! My family life since childhood had been eventful and I learnt many things. When I look up at the night sky and the galaxy beyond, I get overwhelmed and at times forget my own existence, sorrow, frustration and pain. I only become a changed wave in the sea of joy. Did you ever reach your roof top to see the nocturnal sky, sometimes with a binocular, or through the bare eyes? What a great spectacle!

Did you ever see the beauty of the peaceful setting sun? Why should we envy? Why should we fight on this wonderful world? Why should we exhaust our energy on trifles when we have all come down from the omnipotent and fathomless super-intelligent power? Nothing can be destroyed, let alone the lives on earth. No power is combustible. Power can never get exhausted. It changes its shape and form. Longing for life is always there. This inexhaustible eternal longing emerges from eternity. It's supramental. This force is rampant in you and in me. You all have endless indomitable power. Don't depend on your physical limitation. Every man is a superman. But we are always taught otherwise. My father was an exception. As he was a headmaster, a teacher, in our classroom he used to say, "You all possess endless power. You all need proper guidance and inculcation."

Ramakrishna Paramhansa visualized it. So did Christ, Buddha, Albert Einstein. Sometimes we feel dejected seeing our political leaders and travesty of democracy. There should be competitive examinations of competent students in the real sense of the term to study a tough and subtle course to join politics. Failing which we shall get hordes of jokers, bigots and corrupts in our democratic system who have conveniently divided the world into First World, Second World and Third World to make profits. Bertrand Russel though was a non-believer but was one of the greatest champions of world unification and unification of man. He framed 'Foundation' with Einstein and other luminaries to make a salubrious ambience for man's growth and global unification. Like I started 'World Unification League' with my colleagues and students. It was lauded by many plenipotentiaries but ultimately could not move forward owing to downright chauvinism, omnipresent like a monolithic virus in our society. This is a bizarre world. Here Hitler is far better known than Roosevelt, Laden is propagandized more than Nelson Mandela, by media merchants. Do you know today's young generation of England don't know Shakespeare; Roman Rolland is an alien name to the French; Tagore is lost in the limbo of oblivion. One of our former Prime Ministers could not pronounce Alberto Camus when he was delivering a speech in Paris though he had his education in England and belonged to one of the most outstanding cultured families of India.

Fie upon them! Make a long march of love, brotherhood, unification. The connotation of the proverb 'war time footing' always enthuse all of us to pay attention to war and it is making war more popular than peace. This terminology emerges from the deepest corner of our mind for we all love war, war stories, war films, films on destruction and devastation. Which is why our history lacks in information of world lovers, lovers of man. A renowned US President proposed to launch Star Wars! We immediately need Peace to root out terrorism and war. Democracy needs immediate purification. Social scientists should become more meticulous in its application, utilization and modernization. With the advancement of time, democracy and democratic institutions should have been modernized and globalized much before. Bill Gates once stated without knowledge of computers we may be counted as incompetent masses. I love that incompetence but you should not do so. And Bill Gates is a giant of post-modern age. Milan Kundera said, "The light that radiates from the great novels time can never dim, for human existence is perpetually being forgotten by man and thus classics, however old they may be, will never cease to astonish."

More than two thousand years ago in Rome, lepers and prostitutes were either stoned to death or dealt as social outcastes. Jesus was the only savior for these hapless people and he was crucified along with two bandits. But things have changed today. We began loving Jesus and his tenets centuries later. But his mandarins sometimes pose to be stubborn in many aspects which are inhuman. Will our posterity think about our priest craft? And just like humans who were killed once, today we are killing animals in fear of diseases. There is culling of lakhs of chicken ruthlessly to get rid of Bird Flu, are they not eligible to get proper treatment?

2

Each and every individual has an unbound Prometheus within. Let that fire emerge and we can win the universe. Can't we feel that immense power in the paintings of Renoir, Cézanne, Van Gogh, Gauguin, Matisse, Monet, Picasso and Leonardo da Vinci? Did you see the beautiful painting of Matisse of Modern World? It is named 'Dance II'. These astoundingly phenomenal artists desired to change man and the world. They were dreamers. Remember what John Keats said? 'A thing of beauty is joy forever.'

Beautify yourselves, beautify your attire, your home, your neighbourhood, institutions, environment, our Mother Earth and materialize our dreams. What an excellent home we have got in the cataclysm of ever-changing universe! Our society is indirectly driven by ethics of Manu Samhita. I don't know if it is that necessary in today's perspective. In the West and in other societies of the world there was no Manu. Why then women of the world are still kept servile? A lady is constrained to adopt her husband's surname after marriage. This is applicable nearly everywhere all over the world.

My train was running like a gigantic dragon, inside the compartment there is a draconian noise. Am I mad? Why have I resorted to journey without ticket, without food, and without any rhyme and reason? My mother died in her well nurtured servility. After her marriage my father was her Master. When we four brothers grew up, very spontaneously we became her Masters. And she died the most hapless death. Her talent got aborted. My children, cast out your mother's thralldom, cast out women slavery. We must get a far better and beautiful world society where every girl, every woman can think and act freely.

Kasturba Gandhi was given complete freedom by Mahatma so she died with honour and care. In social reformative works she was one of the strongest hands of Gandhiji. Sri Ma of Pondicherry is a great example of woman emancipation. She was a spiritual path finder. Her spiritual master was Sri Aurobindo, not her husband.

I love William Shakespeare's dramas, but I guess he had no conception about ancient India, its beauty, culture, astonishingly beautiful men and women. In the 'Merchant of Venice', in the lottery scene, Bassanio said negatively about Indian beauty, "... veiled Indian beauty. Probably Shakespeare didn't read a single book on India. Cave Paintings of Ajanta was unknown to the world. 'Urvashi' painted on the wall frescos embodies the essence of Indian beauty.

My train has not yet stopped, if it ever stopped, I failed to feel it as I was so absorbed in my writing. No ticket checker came. Through the glass windows, I saw the slow and gradual arrival of dawn.

"Tamasama jyotirgamaya"(The Upanishads)

"There is no darkness but eternal light"

Let us launch a crusade for consciousness bidding adieu to decomposed nationalism, to politicians who are ransacking this planet. Read Russell, Gibran, Tagore. Don't forget to read the Upanishads. Every day we must try to beautify ourselves and Mother Earth. I hope in future and even in the aftermath, our offsprings will not only live under more comfort and security but will successfully utilize dormant vitalities of man. Competition of man is clearly prevalent in violence and war. Power of man shall not be displayed in the battlefields and war. Gandhian non-violence is a great boon, instead of spreading pseudo internationalism, we need to spread the message of love and peace.

War is one of the surprising idiocies of man, and it got the world and society handicapped. Women servility in our planet is a stupidity and it has got our development crippled. There would have been no Karl Marx of 'Das capital' if his wife had not the liberty to guide and advise Marx. Fatima was an integral part of Prophet Mohammed's journey for supramental force and its utilization for the Arabians. There are many such examples.

I am afraid we are not able to find remedies for Cancer. It is enveloping us like infernal cloud and patients die in excruciating pain and trauma. You all must take right measures to abolish this venomous disease from our ill administered planet. I covet a world where there is no cancer, no AIDS, no prostitution, no war, no terrorism, no environmental pollution and no bad politicians. These are equally detrimental in the creation of a graceful world civilization. We discovered Big Bang, Supernova, and we are discovering new galaxies every day. We even hope to get another solar system and solar family in the unending universe. But Cancer hasn't yet got any proper answer. I can only hope that our posterity will be successful in giving the internecine malady a permanent farewell. Man can do everything. We need time and patience. Definitely one of the important causes of this disease is pollution. Who will ask the government of US to stop poisoning the world?

Please don't misunderstand me as I am against age old nationalism. It was an essential aftermath of French Revolution in 1789. After World War II nationalism and political identity have been abused and a deadly weapon race started. But where is the beauty of that borderless world? I am envious of the migratory birds and seafaring animals. A mother tortoise from the Atlantic Ocean comes to the Bay of Bengal to lay eggs. Can I go to Barisal without government infringements!

3

In the early morning, I was intercepted by a ticket collector, and he was naturally very aggressive as I was travelling without a ticket. Then he wanted extra money, which I refused to pay. He suddenly slapped me and it reminded me of how a *panda* of Puri temple had manhandled me years ago. In rage, I slapped him back, but he was a strong man, and caught hold of my shirt's collar. After 15 minutes approximately a station came. It was Samrat Nagar. I was dragged by some GRPs (Railway police) to the station master's room and was remanded for double crime, journeying without ticket and for the counter slap.

My life changed from then on, from a school principal, I became a non-descript thug thrown in a dingy lockup. But I was not perturbed, I again started writing. I was almost possessed. I remembered how Mahatma Gandhi chose to travel in a first-class compartment in South Africa and was thrown out, a victim of apartheid. Yes, I was a rule breaker, I did commit a crime in the eyes of law, and hence was punished. The lockup came as a respite of sorts. I don't know why I chose to plunge into such a life, I kept thinking, like the great thinkers Socrates, Plato and Aristotle did. They could fathom their own power, probably I was waylaid.

Jesus was born with love and non- violence but Buddha and Gandhi earned it. Gandhi reached his culmination through labourious cultivation of mind and Buddha through prolonged penance. If we all become expert cultivators of mind, we shall be able to do magnificent things in various dimensions. Helen Keller was deaf and dumb and blind, yet with help of her teacher Mrs Sullivan, she turned into a prolific writer. Beethoven was deaf, yet he discovered new areas of melody for western classical music. A burglar, a thief, a vagabond like Rousseau, philosophized the world for Human Rights. You all need teachers in real sense of the term. "A station master minds the train and school master trains the mind." Remember Guru Nanak, Kabir, Ramakrishna. Have you read 'Les Miserable' of Victor Hugo? How the great teacher Bishop metamorphosed the thief who entered his house to steal silver candlesticks! I am in the lock up but I am angry with none. I am trying to relinquish anger forever. Do you know what Helen Keller said about us?

"The world has moved along, not only by the mighty shoves of its heroes, but by also by the aggregate of the tiny pushes of each honest worker."

But how to control anger? I was not angry that I was arrested. It seems to be the most difficult task to control. Are we angry when we meet storm, cyclone, tornado, hurricane, earth quake and many other natural catastrophes? Did the helpless victims stand angrily against the tsunami? A man can always be angry with another man or a group but he cannot be angry with inevitability of his death or against nature, for he knows both death and nature are omnipotent. We are afraid of omnipotence. We are always choosy in expressing our wrath. A school teacher can easily be angry with his students but he is seldom angry with the school inspector. He does not dare to be angry! Gandhi could realize the lacuna of anger. So, he could make himself a Mahatma, an eternal icon. Emerson said, "Peace has its victories, but it takes brave men and women to win them." Those braves were Gandhi, Florence Nightingale, St Joan, Father Damien, Baba Amte, Tolstoy, Martin Luther King (Jr.), Nelson Mandela apart from the prophets in the History of man. RW Emerson, Tolstoy, Thoreau were pen gurus of Gandhi during his stay in South Africa. Gandhi changed himself into a colossus of peace and non-violence with the inspirations he had from then in history making correspondence. According to Gandhi, "Poverty is the worst form of violence. What diminishes one of us diminishes us all. But when a person is raised up, to that degree, the whole world is lifted."

Anyway, in the lock up I was served a raw bread and some tea in a clay pot. I was famished and swallowed like a glutton. "The ultimate measure of a man is not where he stands in moments of comfort and convenience, but where he stands at times of challenge and controversy." But we are afraid of that challenge and controversy. When we reach a comfortable and convenient state after prolonged struggle, we do not dare to accept challenge and controversy giving up comfort and convenience. And that is why our civilization suffers, mankind suffers.

"My humanity is bound up in yours, for we can only be human together" --- Archbishop Desmond Tutu had said. But unlike Tutu, there are so many Godmen in every religion who nurture sectarian feelings. My father during his graduation was inspired by Swami Vivekananda and decided to be a sannyasi of the Ramakrishna Mission, but was dissuaded by a Maharaj of the Ramakrishna order. I had Christian friends like Gidion Hudsom Muck from Ohio, brother Prem Sircar, Reverend Henry, Mr Hartnet, Mr Martin and many others. Can any honest man of this planet deny Mother Teresa? Father Hess, the founder of ASISC is a grand old man. He is an embodiment of God. I wrote to Bishop Desmond Tutu several times but unfortunately did not get any reply. But who can defy that great soul?

I slept on the floor of the lock up, I was served no lunch. I felt tired but the hunger was receding gradually. A GRP came and told that I might be sent to the court the next day. I told him that I was a Principal of a Higher Secondary School. I spoke to him in Hindi and English. He was young and robust and felt compassionate. In many countries of the West, prisoners are treated with humanity whatsoever their fault might be, but in India's lock ups, many are ill-treated and many even die. But a criminal is also a human. Think about twenty-seven years' incarceration of Nelson Mandela. Benjamin Moloise, the esteemed young revolutionary poet was hanged by ignoble apartheid government of South Africa. Have you read 'Long Walk to Freedom' by Nelson Mandela? Andre Brick stated about the book ".... burns with luminosity of faith in the invincible nature of human hope and dignity." It is an exciting memoir of an epical character.

It was evening. A dull bulb was nakedly hanging from the ceiling of the lock up. Cobwebs with soot covered the walls. I was so fatigued since the very onset I could not focus my attention on anything, and different thoughts crisscrossed. I remembered Robben Island prison of Nelson Mandela. In my brief trouble I got inspiration from the lives of the greats, films on the greats. Did you see 'Passion of Christ' directed by Mel Gibson? Oh! what a torture Christ had to suffer with love and godliness. Why cannot there be another journey of the Magi? Why cannot there be another heavenly star to show the way to the Magi, to receive another baby in the manger? Where has Jesus gone? Where is Buddha? Can we all not get a ruler like Ashoka? Patrick Lumumba, Salvador Allende, Che Guevara and many others, great souls fought for that cause were killed ruthlessly. Can jails and death penalty be able to remove crime, fictitious move and problems of man?

All the courts of the world can solve problem on ad hoc basis only. Even Oscar Wilde was jailed. DH Lawrence was heckled by lawmakers. Socrates met his death in captivity. Whimsical Pharisee law crucified Jesus. Moody US law killed Che Guevara. And for me? I was in the lock up of Samrat Nagar Rail Station.

As the night descended, that compassionate GRP gave me two bottles of drinking water. Since childhood, I dreamt that one day I would be jailed for serving a great cause, but not for breaking the law. I had no extra shirt with me. I lay on the floor, not at all worried that night for what would happen 'tomorrow'. I did not bother what would happen in court. Most of our present problems are our own creation and there should be pre condition to get rid of this mess. Many astounding discoveries are waiting, many great births shall take place if we don't spoil or destroy this planet by misrule, nasty governance, and parochial judgment.

Within our galaxy, probably there are millions of earths and super earths. If there is no life in our galaxy and anywhere else in the universe then our Mother Earth is the central point of the universe and human being are the prime centre of existence. Can you imagine how important we are then? Don't spoil your valued lives, man is yet to start the task for which he was sent to this planet. Start practising 'Atmanan biddhi' or 'Know thyself.'

As the night gave way to a morning, my sleep broke due to the chirping birds. I woke up and washed myself with the water in the bottles. Toilet in the lock up was far from being a toilet. I was given tea in an earthen pot along with a samosa. The collapsible gate of the lock up was opened and with two GRP men, I was taken to a waiting jeep that rushed towards the Samrat Nagar court. My trial would soon start. In a clumsy dress and a with a tired body, I sat in the jeep. I asked one of my peers: "Is the court very far?" He replied with unwanted gravity, "Approximately twenty-five kilometers." I failed to understand how can the city court be so far away from the railway station.

We finally arrived and I was asked to sit on a bench. Two of my peers talked to an official of sort. Then I was taken inside the court. The judge sat looking dull. I was asked in English whether I needed any lawyer, I refused. I knew my crime, as per law I should be handed down a sentence of three years in jail and I was looking forward to it. At last, would get a chance to write more to my students then!

After the trial, I was taken back to 'Samrat Nagar' prison again. As I walked into the police station's office room, a plump, dark man with small eyes was sitting on an old chair with a worn out table in front of him. Files and papers were scattered. The officer sitting in front of the jeep handed over my papers to him, the GRP men left after wishing me luck. This place would be my home for next three years! All through my odyssey since I came across the ticket checker, I did not understand anything what the others were saying, as they were speaking in their mother tongue and I knew English.

I was given a jail uniform. It was cleaner than my own clothes and henceforth I turned into a number --- number fifteen to be precise. I was confined to a cell, as lunch time was over, I was not served anything to eat. I was given only a bucket of water and tea. After half an hour I went to the bathroom. It was in a pathetic condition. Soot was hanging all around and it smelled of rats. I could see a couple of rhodents around. Once back to my cell, I had long time to sit and think, I was so far away from all of you, my family, my only son, my wife and my friends. I was repenting for being that recalcitrant to board the train without ticket. I was repentant for fighting the duty loving ticket checker. It was a gusty evening. The sky was overcast with dark clouds. All on a sudden it started raining. I was told that the dinner bell would ring at 7pm. And I heard the bell. I was awfully hungry. Many of my inmates were running towards a building inside the jail area with dishes in hand, braving the torrential rain. I managed to walk to the building, and got drenched. The noise made by the inmates was horrendous. I was quite at a loss. My throat and tongue were parched. Most of the inmates were South Indians. As a result, I failed to understand their language. A huge dark inmate came and lifted me up. I requested him in English and then in Hindi and the lifter began talking in a smattering Hindi. When they came to know I was a Bengali, they became joyous and they all danced, lifting me up like a toy. They then put me down. A good cynic like VS Naipaul once compared Bengalis to criminals. And here I was a criminal by the verdict of Law, with other criminals.

I was given two thick, half-burnt chapattis, two hundred grams of rice and sabji. I remembered my hostel days in Mana Camp Boys' Hostel, where the children of the refugees from Bangladesh used to stay. The food in the hostel and here in jail were surprisingly similar. While we were having our dinner, through our conversation in smattering Hindi and English I came to know when prisoners came to this shrine they are called 'amdani', which means import . So, I was like some imported goods to the jail administration. I was offered a single room as I was a school teacher and Principal. I had no book, no paper. Next day, I tried to seek permission from the jail authority to give my diary and pen.

During night a mountain of thoughts traversed through my repentant mind. I felt I should have not done things so hastily and haphazardly. An escapist can never be a good human being. I did not know the real cause of my whimsical move. I wished to return to my students. Gibran said about children like you – "Your children are not your children. They are the sons and daughters of life's longing for itself. They came through you but not from you. And though they are with you yet they belong not to you. You may give them your love but not your thought. For they have their own thoughts. You may house their bodies but not their souls. For their souls dwell in the house of tomorrow which you cannot visit, not even in your dreams."

I silently sobbed. During my hostel life I used to be very homesick. I could not think a moment without my mother. I had similar yearning now, not for my deceased mother, but for all my students. Who I was running away from? Why did I flee? Probably in my subconscious, I wanted to go incognito, I ran away from my love, responsibility and gigantic epoch-making dreams. Now there was no escape, not from this dingy hovel of a jail where I am incarcerated for a grievous fault? How can I synchronize things when I myself am responsible for this mess and confusion? Very likely a confused lunatic like me was not suitable enough to be your teacher in your forthcoming titanic job. May be some great teachers in the real sense of the term, is awaiting you. He shall guide you to perform one of the most astounding phenomenal work in the history of Man and history of the world.

4

Next morning, an official came and started calling our numbers. One of the prisoners was helping him in calling the name. He looked educated and polished. I had to join in the food line, a peculiar edible was hurled in my pot, it was called labsa. I did not know how I swallowed it. In our Mana Camp Boys' Hostel, there was no system of breakfast. After that, during my graduation and post-graduation, I had no money to spend for breakfast. Consequently, I lost the habit of having breakfast.

My work in prison was to teach prisoners. Everything seemed interesting to me. After my night time meal, coming back to my cell I wrote letter to the jailor for supplying me with some books, pens, loose sheets and newspaper. I could not help reiterating that I was a teacher, a principal, an MA in English. I desperately wrote that I was a social reformer, an internationalist, a dreamer, a thinker etc. Oscar Wilde who was imprisoned for being a homosexual, got agitated when he was jailed. He referred to the blue tent of the jail as the sky. At all odds, I too got accustomed to the life in prison. I was allowed to get an English newspaper every day along with three dot pens and paper. I began doing exercise in my space-crunched cell. Some of my comrades were fairly educated and we became friends. In the evenings many of them had visitors, and every evening I waited, but none came.

I thought about Napoleon Bonaparte who was metamorphosed into a great man from a proud imprisoned emperor during his long exile in St Helena Island. In St Helena he was privileged to be addressed 'emperor' by all as per the royal verdict of Great Britain. One morning he was walking with two British guards, when a black African boy, a helpless slave, was passing by him with big logs of woods on his head. "Did you not see the emperor is walking, you black boy?" One of the white guards stormed at him. Napoleon replied, "Why are you shouting at him? He is also a human like you and me." Many great men became greater during their imprisonment.

After demise of my beloved mother and my much-adored father, I began sliding away from my family and relatives. Now I dreamt of all of them in the prison. My son was also my student, though I was always an unimportant teacher to him. I thought to apply to the Jail Super to inform everyone at last about my whereabouts, but I could not. Some jail inmates were homosexuals. Young people used to be victims by the seniors and some complained to me fully knowing well that I was a teacher. I disliked bullying of any kind and was furious, going against the sex goondas in jail. I protested vehemently against this sexual abuse during dinner. Some youngsters were with me and they all shouted with me. The senior ring leaders did not reply or pay any attention. I told them I would convey the matter to the jail authority. I wrote to the super, but no action was taken. Conversely, I was reprimanded by a jail official. He reminded me that I was also a convict and I should not forget my own identity in the jail. In accordance with them I was in no way eligible to complain.

One fine morning after breakfast we were asked to enjoy, as it was a national holiday. I went out and looked at the sky when two goons came and started doing caricature of me. I got angry and shouted at them, "What fucking things are you doing?" They instantly pounced upon me and kept kicking me. I was almost faint with pain. The emergency bell was rung. The guards came and rescued me. My face was swollen, my nose was bleeding, and every bone in my body was aching excruciatingly. None of the youngsters who protested earlier with me came to my rescue. I was trying to stand up but kept falling down. An old stretcher was brought and I was taken to my cell where the jail doctor came to check. The doctor advised to get me admitted to the jail hospital as my left arm was probably broken.

Probably I was half unconscious and when I came back to my right sense, I found myself bandaged and plastered. At the hospital doctors and nurses were conversant in English. They took good care of me. A sympathetic nurse looked after me. Her name was Kavita. She told me, "You look like my father." And she became like a daughter to me. Mr Ravi was my doctor. These medics brought about a new dimension in my jail life and I began forgetting I was a criminal too. Fighting within the jails is a phenomenon in our so-called post-modern civilization. Jails have to be transformed into holy shrines where criminals and so-called criminals would get ample scope to reform. This old and absurd 'Lex Talionis', the law of the world has to be relinquished. Even Harry Truman, the then President of USA ravaged Hiroshima and Nagasaki, appreciated the laboratories of US manufacturing the worst weapon to kill man. Jails are places where everyone is confined. But look at the migratory birds: they are the real symbols of internationalism and freedom. Or even the marine life. Their world is bigger than our land mass. And they are free and international. Leaders like Harry Truman created terrorism of today due to their vindictive attitude. If my point is true then I should say I was in jail within the jails. Every nation piles up weapons from a sense of insecurity. Who will bell the cat when power corruption is frolicsome? Lord Acton once stated, "Power corrupts and absolute power corrupts absolutely."

In the hospital I was allowed to read newspaper by the mercy of Dr Ravi. I came to know Dr Binayak Sen, the human rights activist was selected for this year's Dr Jonathan Mann Award for global health and Human Rights. Even his bail plea has been turned down. He was arrested branding him a dreaded Naxalite under Special Security Act that empowers the Indian Police to arrest and detain anyone for an indefinite period without trial. No incriminating thing was discovered during the search of his house. His trial is excessively delayed. "Justice delayed is justice denied." He is in a solitary confinement for a year. His wife Ilina Sen appealed to the Supreme Court but Hon'ble Supreme Court dismissed the petition in one sentence only.

In 2004 Christian Medical College of Vellore was extremely proud when Dr Sen was given the Paul Harrison Award. In 2007 the Indian Academy of Social Sciences awarded him with RR Keithon Gold Medal for his brilliance and brilliant social service. He was the National Vice President of People's Union for Civil Liberties (PUCL) and the General Secretary of Chattisgarh chapter. He was an Assistant Professor in Jawaharlal Nehru University. He later joined Shankar Guha Neogi of Chhattisgarh Muktimorcha. Guha Neogi was killed. They were against tremendous exploitation of the adivasis by the godheads of Chhattisgarh. Shankar Guha Neogi married an adivasi lady. When my father was in Pakhanjore of Chhattisgarh both Guha Neogi and his wife met him for advice welfare. Dr Sen along with his friends opened an NGO Rupantar and established a hospital of 25 beds for the poorest of the poor. It was owned and run by the workers. Starvation, illiteracy, and lack of livelihood devastated the lives of the tribes in Chhattisgarh. Market driven development is still making their lives miserable. Indiscriminate arrests, rape, physical and mental torture, deaths in police custody and encounter are rampant in the name of combating 'Maoists.'

During his stay in jail Dr Binayak Sen lost 20kgs. The outstanding Latin American revolutionary Che Guevara was killed by Cuban American CIA agents. When he was arrested in a jungle of Bolivia he said, "I know you have come to kill me. Shoot coward. You are only going to kill a man." Every kind of killer in the world is a coward. It is ridiculous that democracy gave us more hatred and violence. Democracy is the best method no doubt. But it needs purgation world over.

I was gradually improving in the hospital and learnt my imprisonment term has been extended. Kavita was extremely sorry for this extension. Nobody was there to appeal for me. Still, I did not forget my dream. I told everything to Dr Ravi and Kavita. They were curious to know many more things but did not dare give me any assistance for I was a criminal. My dream is an epical one – to unite the world through love and non-violence and to end once and for all, the poverty, injustice and petty nationalism that had bled the world for centuries.

A few days later, a fitness certificate was issued and I was directly taken in a police jeep with armed guards. I was taken far away from the previous jail and hospital. At the time of my departure, I could not meet Kavita, my motherly young nurse. Again, two hours later, our jeep stood in front of a gigantic concrete wall and massive iron gate. They dragged me ruthlessly as if I was an animal to be butchered. Ravi's information was correct. A jail official read a report in English which asserted that I was a Naxalite. In fact, they had my case history since I was arrested and thrown behind iron gates that were impenetrable. My life would change forever.

Chapter 12
Search for the Divine Soul

1

The jail life now was torturous, yet I learnt to be tolerant. The only sounds I was exposed to were a faraway dog's nocturnal wailing, shrill calls of night birds, squeaking of rats, lizards tick tacking. All my hopes were gradually dying. Children, I was afraid lest I turn into a lunatic. I dealt with my life maddeningly and I failed to create anything. But didn't Van Gogh create his masterpieces with maddening passion, Shelley was addressed as 'Mad Shelley' in college.

In my cell I had only a small window and the barber gave me a shave. Only a bucket of water was given for my ablution and bath. It reminded me of jail life of Sri Aurobindo, the great rishi. Meals were tasteless stuff, I had no chance to read newspapers or listen to radio. TV was out of question. My mental condition was gradually ameliorating. As days passed, the jail authorities probably realized I was not any notorious terrorist and gave me a pen and a pad to write and I was even allowed to go out of the cell in the evening. One morning after having my bath of sort, I was chanting Gayatri mantra aloud and a guard was moved by my chanting. He praised me highly, his name was TVK Rao. We began to develop a friendship, his father was a primary school teacher and he learnt English.

The jail authorities thought I was a Naxal. So during my evening walks, two guards escorted me. TVK Rao did not come daily, but I waited for him. When he came, he discussed about news of the outside world. When I expressed, I was keen on reading newspapers and books, he said he would try to bring me some newspapers. Meanwhile I was taken to the court but I had none to plead my cause. I did not lose hope. Nelson Mandela was my role model. I nurtured a belief that my penance in jail would give me spiritual strength and it would help the inmates of the world of sufferers for redemption. TVK told me to apply to Raman Subba Rao, the jail super regarding reading privileges. I wrote and my application was honoured. On World Environment Day, I came to know Barrack Obama outplayed Hillary Rodham Clinton in the election race to claim the nomination from Democratic Party in US Presidential election. In fact, Barrack crossed the threshold for his party's Presidential nomination. I felt after Kennedy USA got a real internationalist with generosity. But he might in the long run promise like chauvinists for vote banks. To salvage the globe from multiple destructions, Obama, Nelson Mandela, Bill Gates, Noam Chomsky and Al Gore should think and work together. It felt as if Barrack Obama was the dream child of Martin Luther King (Jr).

Rao told me during my evening stroll that two hijras were brought to the seclusive cell for they were stubborn Naxalites. I shuddered. In our country and in many countries of the world they are abhorred and hated. They are taunted, flayed, misbehaved with and castigated, as if they are social outcastes. Recently some organizations are fighting for them. Many years ago, an American young man happened to meet me; he was doing an extensive research work on hijras. He questioned me about their problems and why were they neglected and treated with ruthless hatred. I could not answer. I got to know that both eunuchs were inmates of Chhattisgarh and they were being trained by the Naxal leaders.

I loathed violence, killing, genocide, bloodshed and war. Our life time is very short. Violence and killings are making man's life shorter. Our globe is entirely enveloped by violence, wars, terrorism, massacres, hatred, conspiracy and corruption. Even Einstein's great discovery was abused by Openheimer Project. Violent leaders are always worshipped by the nations. God is in every man. In one way or the other every person in the world has been in the quest of supreme power. Every kind of philosophy, scientific discoveries, theism, monotheism and atheism surfaced for that urge only. Emperor Constantine after adopting Christianity began killing the non-Christians in accordance with the instruction of the church. Consequently, Roman Empire had its downfall. Could we get a super-giant lover of man like Jesus instead?

I was delighted to know from a newspaper given to me by Rao, that hundreds of activists from a broad coalition of almost 50 international Human rights groups consists of Amnesty

International, National Lawyers' Guild, South Asian Network thronged together for secularism and democracy. Canada protested on the streets on two global days of action against the continued incarceration of human rights crusader Dr Binayak Sen. Similar protests were held in front of Indian Consulates in London, New York, Washington DC, San Francisco and Vancouver. While professors in Paris, Stockholm, Boston, Pittsburgh, Houston and many other cities held talks and film screenings to raise awareness about the incessant persecution of human rights activists. More than 4,000 signatures from around the world were collected on petitions asking Dr Sen's emancipation from incarceration. Intellectuals of global standard including Noam Chomsky, George Galloways along with many Indian intellectuals jointly urged the government of India to release Dr Binayak Sen. Twenty-two Nobel Prize Scientists and economists appealed to our government to release him and allow him to go in person to receive the 2008 Jonathan Mann award for health and Human Rights in Washington.

Dr Sen is the fifth person to have been arrested under CSPSA in the state. He was arrested on fictitious charges of sedition on 13th May, 2007 along with many other human rights activists. They are charged under repressive "Black Laws," the government got chagrined with him as he vehemently protested against "Salwa Judum" a private militant move patronized by Chhattisgarh government to combat insurgency of the Maoists. Our democratic values succumbed to the Emergency period of 1975.

Subhash Chandra Bose is addressed as 'Netaji'. To our utter dismay we get innumerable so called Netajis today. How can one of the greatest patriots of the history of this planet be commonly known as 'neta' only, when 'Neta' now seems to be a filthy term. Subhash Bose had left his Elgin Road house in Calcutta in disguise, after reaching Afghanistan with Mr. Habibur Rehman, he had another sobriquet. It was Ziauddin Ahmed. He had a shelter in the house of Uttam Chand. Chandra Bose (as he was known to the Europeans and Americans) left for the then USSR as an Italian. Now he was Arlanda Mazzito. He sported a French cut beard. He was totally baffled with Stalin and journeyed to Germany and met Hitler. From Germany he boarded a submarine with Habibur. After a prolonged and traumatic journey, he reached Japan and met Marshal Tojo, the premier.

He had the captaincy of Indian National Army formed by Rashbehari Bose and he renamed it as Azad Hind Fauj. That very Fauj conquered erstwhile Burma and reached Imphal to hoist the Indian National Flag but ultimately lost in the limbo of oblivion. I believe had he stayed long in the world he could have become one of the greatest internationalists. History is acquainted with his patriotism but his best kernel is unknown. We are unfortunate that he and the Mahatma could not work together. He like Che-Guevara fought the battle of independence from outside the country. While Che fought for communism, Subhash fought for the independence of his mother land. But the difference lay in the fact that while Che was a communist, Subhash Chandra Bose was staunch lover of Ramakrishna, the embodiment of the universe.

During my graduation years in Raipur, I was influenced by Sitansu Misra, Prantosh Chatterjee, Vaskaran Nair, CV, Joy and Miss Apparao to join the Naxal Movement in Chhattisgarh. It was then in a prenatal stage. At that time, I had no knowledge of Gandhiji, I knew nothing about Nelson Mandela. I had no interest in Abraham Lincoln. Martin Luther King (Jr.) was just a name to me. I read red Books of Mao Zedong, I read Che, Lenin and Marx rudimentarily. We had a secret place for meetings that were conducted at night. I was hypnotized by Mao's personality and believed in his prescribed path of violence. Miss Appa Rao was innovative and she was my Guru. I admired her. I was a fan of Mary Tyler of Jaduguda.

But nobody in the group believed in the Almighty, the universal cosmic force in which I had absolute faith. They did not love spiritualism and had minimum respect for the heritage of India and of the world. Killing was their only path for success. As a result, I got gradually disillusioned. Chhattisgarh was one of the pivotal centres of exploitations of the poor. I argued with many a brilliant scholar regarding violence, killing and massacre. They with their brilliant scholarship defeated me easily in our bickering. I did not dare open my lips with Apparao lest she might take me otherwise. My father made a prognosis in 1976, "...If adivasis in our areas are exploited likewise there shall be violence and killings within three decades."

Probably I would someday come out of jail and enlighten the world with the movement of love. If I fail, after my death you students must move, not with violence but with love. You must fight in a novel way against corruption, exploitation and improper distribution of power and wealth. All religions of the world, books and philosophies of the world are spruced up for man's progress and global improvement. India lost its original character since it's partition in 1947. Similarly, China lost its classical and spiritual dimension since 1949. Both countries had intercourse of culture, education and spiritualism for couple of centuries and glorious civilizations. Now both are nurturing animosity at the cost of love, brotherhood, amalgamation of spiritualism and culture.

It is unfortunate that China is no more a proper democracy. Sun Yat Sen is not remembered at least by the Government of China since its very inception as Red China. Soul of Indian civilization lies in Pakistan. It is the shrine of Indus Valley Civilization. It is well known that before the beginning of the world navigation, foreigners would migrate through Khyber Pass and Bolan Pass. Now both the passes are situated in Pakistan. In British India, Hindus and Bengali Hindus were patronized for British safety and security. Britishers usurped India from the rulers of India. And most of the Indian rulers were Muslims. Consequently, they patronized Indian aristocrats excluding Muslims. The sequel of which was India's bifurcation.

The relation between India and USA have always been a roller coaster ride. In spite of prolonged political hiatus since Nehru and Eisenhour, friendship between the people of both the countries is laudatory. Many years ago, Swami Vivekananda, launched his dynamic society making race by American cooperation and patronization. In the aftermath many Ramakrishna cult sannyasis made USA their second home. Jiddu Krishna Murthy, Prabhupad of ISCON, Kriyayogi Swami Jogananda and many other spiritual leaders of India were discovered by USA. Failure of mere Indo-American agreement or 'Nuke Deal' should not rupture the love and brotherhood we shared. Both Lyndon Johnson and Richard Milhouse Nixon were not efficacious to destroy this tie. Agreements and treaties are there in the world for faithlessness and disbelief. Artificial friendship dies a natural death. America since the period of Eisenhour enveloped Pakistan with that artificial friendship and Pakistan's permanent democracy is still a burning question. Pakistan has had the worst tragedy in the Post World War II era. Muhammad Ali Jinnah died in 1948 and the Pakistan of

Kyed E Azam succumbed instantly. Mr Jinnah was a maverick in the Congress for Indian Independence. Liaquat Ali was killed, Z A Bhutto was hanged and Benazir lost her life. The masses in Pakistan are misled.

In April 1947 Gandhi proposed to install Jinnah as the Prime Minister of undivided India – a united India. Horrified Congress rejected the plan. It was definitely a Herculean blunder. Gandhi could have saved India from total mess caused by bifurcation. Gandhi also believed in one world. He said, "A friend asked yesterday, did I believe in one world?" Of course, I believe in one world. And how can I possibly do otherwise? ......you can redeliver that message now in this age of democracy, in the age of awakening of the poorest of the poor." This speech was made to a gathering of Asian leaders.

Gandhi said at one point in the April 1947 speech, possibly referring to the violence of the Great War II, the holocaust of the Semitic race, holocaust in the Hindu Muslim riot.

"I am sorry to have to say that but it is my feeling.... the West today is pining for wisdom. The best today is despairing of multiplication of atom bombs because multiplication of atom bombs means utter destruction, not thereby of the West, as if the prophecy in the bible is going to be fulfilled, and there is to be a perfect deluge." He spoke on behalf of the vast number of people who lived in India in dire poverty. He said after nuclear holocaust in Hiroshima and Nagasaki: "What I want you to understand – if you can – that the message of the East, the message of Asia, is not to be learned through Western spectacles, not by imitating the tension of the West, the gunpowder of the West the atom bomb of the West" He further told his listeners, "If you want to give message again to the West, it must be a message of love; it must be a message of truth, there must be a conquest..." His words were cut off with applause by a rousing cheer. Characteristically Gandhi said, "Please, please, please that will interfere with my speech and that will interfere with your understanding also. I want to capture your hearts, and don't want to receive your claps. Let your hearts clap in unison with what I am saying, and think I shall have finished my work."

Dear children,

Always remember and chant, *"Iswar Allah tero naam/sabko sanmmati de Bhagwan."*

Romain Rolland always coveted for new light and excellent spiritual message from the East, from India. Message of Buddhism, Confucianism, message from the Vedas and Vedantas along with the message of Gandhi will dawn a new era. Gandhi was inspired by the Ramayana and the Bible. They sometimes left message for us which seems identical.

Man, of today or tomorrow needs Global Legislation to combat terrorism. Terrorists are privileged with GPS, cell phones and internet and the most advanced weapons. Even the most powerful nations cannot work out a solution. The whole world must work together. Like Gandhi said: "Be the change you want in the world."

Remember my children, terrorism is giving a bad name to religion. That was why John Lennon sang "Imagine there is no country….no religion too." Radical religion turns philosophies into orthodoxy. To cleanse the Augean stable of the world, youth awakening is quintessential. Failing which we shall have no choice but be snuffed out. We are awaiting the Youth Revolution throughout the Globe. Definitely we shall have to change ourselves to change the world.

2

The new jail super Mr Patnari did not like me. I got emaciated, frail and weak, I wore a long beard and moustache, like actor Steve McQueen's role in the blockbuster Hollywood film 'Papillon'. Oh! What a hardship the prisoner underwent! Can we the citizens of the world improve lives in prisons of the world! Can we not reform our legal system along with reforming the world! All the pending files of legal system of our country can reach the height of Mt Everest several times. I wanted a copy of the Gita, Mr Patnari allowed me one. I was given a copy of the Gita, the holy Bible and the holy Quran. Presumably they found a positive change of a Naxalite from atheism to theism. Tagore cried in many of his poems in pangs to almighty to usher a change. Swami Vivekananda gave a powerful call against priestcraft. But these great men's legacies are misused and exploited. Tagore once wrote that Buddha, Jesus failed and Gandhi would also fail. Look at Gandhi's posterity in India and in the world. Are they not corrupt jokers? Real jokers are never corrupt. Remember Charlie Chaplin.

Every morning, I read the Gita, during afternoons I read the holy Bible and at night time I read the holy Quran in my hellish cell. My hell was no longer a hell to me. I cried for my father and my mother. Three best guiding books of the world of all time were with me. I could sometimes even feel my mother's presence in the room. The ecstasy is indescribable. I was now a proud prisoner. Gradually I began loving my prison life, a lizard was my room partner. A sparrow sometimes came to haunt my lonely cell. TVK Rao and other guards told me that I looked like a mendicant.

In early seventies I was going to Pakhanjore, my father's place, from my hostel during Puja vacation. I got down at Kanker to change my bus, for I boarded the bus from Raipur, it was a red bus of the erstwhile Madhya Pradesh Government. When I went to collect the ticket, the robust owner of 'Anand Transport' came to sell the tickets from a hut. Some poor coolies were relaxing on the floor of the hut. That robust Anand Transportwala said," Hash! Hash! chal! chal!" as if he was chasing out some street dogs from the open hut of his father. The poor porters did not even show any sign of vexation. They left the place immediately.

Remember the demon created by Dr. Frankenstein of Mary Shelley, the doctor died deliberately with his creation, the demon, due to the demon's destructive attitude. The destructive attitude of the governance of every country, the same of the politicians and their brainless muscle men, attitude of the fanatics, and of the terrorists may compel the Mother Earth to commit suicide with all of us if we fail to kill her by dint of our longstanding downright idiocy. Nature's anger is devastating. Mother Earth is an embodiment of nature.

I had a stomach trouble for the last two days. But neither was I given proper medicine nor proper care. I am a patient of gastritis and chronic dysentery. I developed it during my stay in Mana Camp Refugee Hostel. My diet there was just the same. I shall not be able to be proud of this jail life. I am afraid; I am not that worthy to be in a cell like the living legend of the world like Nelson Mandela. He is my inspiration, my role model. I cannot understand how my life's route did not run according to my dream.

Neither apoliticians nor politicians shall individually be able to bring about a new world order, new world government or a government of a super state. The name of the super state is the 'world'. I was influenced by my father to think myself a citizen of the world. I was really overwhelmed when Aparna Sen, a great director pronounced with pride that she considered herself a citizen of the world. But is there anybody to accord us world citizenship? We need spiritual awakening at every corner of the world. No cult, no religion, no 'ism' of the past will be able to change the scenario. Concept of deep-rooted nationalism shall ultimately jeopardize our existence and health of this planet. It is far more vituperative than cancer, HIV/AIDS and terrorism.

I was a laughing stock to many in the eighties, when I tried to inculcate the necessity of world unification. But I believe my Mother Earth is able to feel my sentiment. She is allowing me to think and feel that way. I believe within 21st century all the nations of the world shall be united, terrorists shall be given eternal Farewell and so shall be done by the nations and fanatics. In such a critical juncture patriotism and fanaticism are obverse and reverse of a single coin. Our periphery of thought has to be lengthened to a remarkable extent. Our preposterous scientific inventions and its misappropriation are ailing this planet. She needs proper diagnosis and treatment. Man always needs an adversary to work on war time footing. Onslaught of natural calamity, catastrophe, tsunami, impact of HIV/AIDs cannot stop us from leading a Global Unification Movement. And nation states are impertinently dashing this globe to that alarming arena. World Federation shall be the first step to ascend with total civilization of man.

My children! My students! My sons and daughters, you start worshipping our lovely planet, before you worship, chant hymns for the almighty. Don't you hear our mother Earth is groaning in trauma? She needs care, nursing, love, and proper panacea for recuperation and good health for better tomorrow. Condemn unitedly the 'Manhattan Project" guided and run by R.Openheimer, the scientific director of this globetrotting ignoble project. He is called 'Father of world's first atom bomb.' It is told that Openheimer was influenced by Bhagvad Gita and was mesmerized by Chapter 17' Sraddhatrayamory Yoga' and he possessed an original Sanskrit Gita in his desk inside the Los Memos Bomb Laboratory. He used to browse upon it intermittently. But one of the greatest peacemaker Mahatma Gandhi was influenced by Gita to such an extent that he addressed it 'Mother'. Einstein once said, "Science without religion is lame. Religion without science is blind." But men like Openheimer are always lame and blind. He said after 6th August 1945 "I did my job which I was supposed to do. I was not in a policy making position. I would have done anything that I was asked to do."

Last night I was vomiting blood in toilet of my cell. Every joint of my body ached severely. Probably I was attacked with arthritis. Even my poor body is a temple of living God. I used to complain about insomnia. I was habituated to sleeping pills, but here in the jail, I was not allowed to have any. I spent sleepless nights.

The World Wars had divided this planet into clans, sects, communities, fanning enmity and hatred of surmounting proportion and finally jeopardized human existence. Kaiser Wilhelm of Germany said, "If we don't get colony in the world we will carve out colony in the Sun." But consider the present world leaders, are they any better? APJ Abdul Kalam, our ex-president, a great man, emerged as a father figure of India's nuclear energy after Pokhran Nuclear Test on 11 August 1998. How did this great scientist work like Openheimer? But then again his greatness was manifested after he became President of India. Had Kalam remained president for a longer duration, India might have been blessed better in words and action. But my concern is not India only. I dream like John Lennon. I did not find any in our time who loved man and Mother Earth. Definitely you remember his song --

Imagine there's no heaven,
It's easy if you try,
No hell below us,
Above us only sky,
Imagine all the people
living for today...

Imagine there's no countries,
It isn't hard to do,
Nothing to kill or die for,
No religion too,

Imagine all the people
living life in peace...

John Lennon tried to reform everything by his enchanting songs. He was killed in 1980. Patriotism and religion, as a matter of fact is the root cause of genocide and destruction. Patriotism as per its own system turns into chauvinism and religion ultimately creates fanatics. In the Jagannath Temple of Puri, a European had happened to enter and the prasadam cooked for thousands was thrown in the gutter and the temple was washed for purification. If for the *Brahmanda* there is a single omnipotent god, how for every sect there can be many gods? It is said 'Eshwar ekamebadwitiam' , 'sarabkhalledum brahma', parambrahma, the supermost power of the universe is ubiquitous everywhere. I was willing to visit Mecca during Haj but I will never be allowed for my sect. Our Mother Earth is a small planet like a petite and most beautiful queen of the universe, but we are fragmenting it. The widely honoured Swedish poet Tomas Transtromer wrote: "......the world is one. But walls.... And the world is a part of yourself – Whether you know it or not it's the same for everyone /everyone except the little children. No walls for them."

Don't you dream of man's progeny reaching neighbouring planets to make our homes? When our scientists are bringing about astounding discoveries, we should dream likewise. The greatest scientists of the world always have thought big. The search for the God's particle or Higgs Boson particle has yielded success. The launch of the large Harden Collider at CERN in Geneva allowed some real intelligent people to say that the 'Doomsday is in the offing.' When the nuclear fuel of the core is exhausted, gravity can cause the contract over highest densities. The mechanism for forming super massive black holes of millions and billions of solar masses is not yet understood though it may very likely involve the merger of smaller black holes and the intake of surrounding stars and gas.

In December 1929, our great scientist Satyendranath Bose had proposed a new way of classifying particles according to their distributions in energy. It is the basis of Bose and Einstein statistics. A proton beam was switched on so much so that collisions have to wait the counter beam to switch on next month. The present day Large Hadron Collider shall be used for four major experimentations including the search for the Higgs Boson dark matter, anti-matter, the Quark-gluon plasma that formed immediately after the Big Bang. Stephen Hawking had a prognosis that these will evaporate in a fraction of a second leaving behind a telltale flash of Hawking radiation, but he also gave a single percent chance of occurring. The collision of the two protons is estimated to produce about one lakh times the energy of the Sun's core.

But before reaching other planets we have got to be unified into a single unit of human race. There is only one nation in the world and that is Human Nation. The greatest contribution was made to our planet by great scientists, but their excellent creations were mostly misused and manhandled. Years ago, a number of Nobel laureate scientists expressed their pain with Gunter Gras. "It's our misfortune that most of our so-called leaders of the world are immature, haughty, unintelligent and impertinent. Which is why progress in science and progress of mind did not work in coordination. Time is ripening and man has got to think otherwise. Failing which our planet shall be a roving sepulcher round the sun." In July 1945 at the Potsdam Conference, Stalin told Churchill and Truman, "The death of one man is tragedy. The death of millions a statistic." On the other hand, in 1945 Einstein stated after USA bombed Hiroshima and Nagasaki "The release of atom power has changed everything....... the solution to this problem lies in the heart of mankind. If only I had known, I should have become a watch maker."

You must read 'Gulag Archipelago' of Aleksandr Solzhenitsyn and 'Anne Frank's Diary'. Dictators of the world created anathema unabashedly. USA resorted to extinguish Vietnam and then the world cried, Europe cried, Jean Paul Sartre a colossal writer and philosopher of France protested, Beatles protested with their songs. General Macarthur monitored the atom bomb holocaust in Japan and in the aftermath, he talked like a great philosopher in his interviews. Is he not the one of the worst hypocrites of the world? Why shall we not compare him and his lieutenants with Osama Bin Laden? I can hear the wailing of the souls of Hiroshima and Nagasaki victims, listen to the vehement groaning of millions massacred in Nazi concentration camps, feel the pangs of billions tortured by our frenzied governments.

3

Children, don't misunderstand my frustration in democracy. It is the most powerful weapon for mankind. It can only do away with arms; can only fulfil every kind of dream for shaping a positive world. Democracy gave rise to science, technology, literature, poems, songs, music, art films, and gave the option of choosing our own gods. But those who monitor democracy in countries are not thinking at all for mankind. Without proper training, none should have been allowed to give captaincy in democracy. Everyone is not Abraham Lincoln, FD Roosevelt, Kennedy or Lal Bahadur Sastri. I discovered the outstanding best democracy in the universe, in the heavenly bodies, in stars, in galaxies.

Afro-American Barrack Hussein Obama was sworn in as the 44th President of the most powerful nation of the world. He is the first American President to mention 'Hindus and non-believers' in his inaugural speech. As a citizen of the world, I appreciated his impeccable and minute observations. His father was from Kenya and mother was white American. A new chapter in the world history opened thus. He told in his world famous speech, "We are shaped by every language and culture drawn from every end of this earth; and because we have tasted the bitter swill of civil war and segregation and emerged from the darker chapter stronger and more united, we cannot help but believe that the old hatreds someday pass; that the lines of tribe shall soon dissolve that as the world grows smaller, our common humanity shall revive itself; ushering in a new era of peace." I feel once out of Oval office people like Obama should serve again. The world needs leaders like him, he can be the best to spearhead towards world peace. The traumatic problem of worldwide terrorism is a burning question. Should we only wait and watch? Let us all join together to free the world from the terrorists and ignoble terrorism of worst type. Terrorism dawned in 1914 by killing Archduke Ferdinand and the duchess. Later ambitious politicians' callousness and foolhardy attitude let it grow. During Cold War, it was patronized by the then super powers. All over the world UN acts poorly with weak Secretary Generals excluding Dag Hammarskjold. I entreat all the students of the world to go ahead without political parochialism to make the world a free world in real sense of the term. Terrorism is the worst curse after the blunt and brainless cold war. Fascism and Nazism once were eulogized, applauded and accepted. Stalin, Churchill and Roosevelt were silent spectators when Hitler and Mussolini were growing and ravaging like hobgoblins. Churchill cherished and nurtured the idea of British colonialism and even referred Gandhi as 'half naked Indian fakir' and none did protest.

Van Gogh once painted a tree, that grew into a mammoth tree, crossing the sky, the moon, the sun, the stars and other heavenly bodies. He fathomed man's omnipotent power and expressed it by the tree he painted. Man can create, invent, discover anything and everything. If man can create hecatombs in Hiroshima Nagasaki, in Vietnam, in Nazi concentration camps, on the destruction of Bamian Buddhas, in the building in Afghanistan and in Palestine, and in many other places, then why shall he not be as great as the tree portrayed by Van Gogh, if he thinks positively, optimistically, spiritually and with love. We need self-sacrifice, unfailing honesty and sometimes splendid obsession which reject private sorrow and private failures like empty shells. We must have a generous impulse to contribute to the world everything that is fine and vital in our minds and hearts though, our life may appear hard and agonizing, our path must be joyous. Develop minds of artists. Are you not amazed at nature's ability to create flawless colour combination, the infinite variety of their shades and the colouring of the Earth that changes constantly but is equally beautiful in every moment and in all seasons! Van Gogh believed that a great future waited for work man, poet and scholars.

My jail life for no fault of my own is becoming painful. Cellular jail of Andaman and Nicobar Island was the worst jail of our sub-continent during the British Raj. I heard it from Greta. Had I been there I would have died much earlier. Prisons of our country should have been improved by governments decades ago. If we do not take right measures to bring prison management in tune with time and with our judicial system, then social hazards will increase. All the jails are overcrowded, many are languishing without trial and some do suffer life behind the bars for long even after they are acquitted for lack of coordination between court and jail administration. Many are denied the basic rights, on the contrary there are convicts who contest elections! They are the political goons. Our total system is plagued with incompetence and prisons have been impacted notoriously.

Meanwhile, Mr Mukhtar Ahmed joined as new jail super. He met me personally. He was a 'paanch waqt namazi' Muslim, much younger than me. His every word emanated from his pure soul. I chanted from the holy 'Chandi' in Sanskrit. He chanted from the holy Koran. Oh! What a great pleasure! He was godsent. He allowed me to get two English newspapers regularly along with three weekly English journals. He promised he would try for my release. I was given better diet and medicines. Meanwhile in my year-long jail life, I developed severe migraine and eye trouble. I did not complain of it to Mukhtar sahib. Two more officers were sympathetic to me. They were Mr Reddy and Mr Ramaswamy. Probably they heard about me from Mukhtar sahib. In our third meeting I began addressing him as Mukhtar bhai.

Later on, I came to know that he is a bosom friend of Piramanayangam, my student, who passed the ICSE examination in 1984, innovative and brilliant and went to South India to be an IPS. He did not know my whereabouts but happened to talk about me to Mukhtar bhai. From him I managed to know that Piramanyangam was at present posted in Delhi and had many medals from the President of India.

It is dead of night. The dull and shaded light came up. I was warned by a guard to go to bed by 7pm and I complied with his request. After all I am in a prison, a criminal in the hands of law. Next morning, I applied to the jail super to get me permission to write at night. Three days after Mukhtar bhai came with permission. I was overwhelmed and jumped to embrace him forgetting my own identity in the jail. I got to know that Piramanayangam would be holidaying in Chennai shortly and he was keen on meeting me. He knew from Mukhtar bhai that I was in jail as an anti-national political prisoner. I waited eagerly. I wrote a letter to him in which I wrote about Mrs Apparao, my serious and proud friend during my schooling in Communism, Marxism and Mao-zedong's thoughts. I was influenced by her but in the aftermath, I got disillusioned for I hate killing, murder, massacre, war, guns, bullets, and all lethal weapons.

Our intelligence is growing, sensitivity is growing but our society is dull. It cannot create an intelligent world. Every sanguinary movement is a crime, an infernal crime. Sometimes I think this mess in the world society and on the earth, itself can never be rectified unless we start it again from primitive stage. Great men, philosophers, thinkers, god men, failed to repair it either for their incapacity or incapacity of our own. Our world society has been neurotic almost from the very inception. Our history is replenished with violence, destruction, war, artificiality and lunacy. So, we are taught from our childhood to say, "My country is the greatest country in the world. My religion is the greatest religion in the world." For this neurotic disorder in our social system, we have become dull and insensitive. But a single man's potential is abysmal, like a single seed of a tree. A single seed gives birth to a massive tree and it gives birth to innumerable seeds. These innumerable number of seeds give birth innumerable trees and ultimately a single seed can cover up the entire world with greenery. Every man is a miracle. That same miracle is there in you, in me, in the forthcoming each and every man individually. Realizing our pathetic and traumatic condition in the world society for thousands of years Emerson wrote, "Man is God in ruins." It is uncontroversially true, but every ruin can be revamped. We all must individually try to get rid of this ruinous state and discover our reality from the ruins, our omnipotence, and our dormant and latent omniscience, our consciousness.

I believe there are many in this world who are thinking to launch a global movement like me. The Mahatma in his book 'My Truth' did not refer to the Absolute Truth. With a view to making himself a perfect man he experimented with his celibacy. Pandit Nehru said, "Absolute Truth is beyond our means." Truth is beautiful. John Keats said, 'Beauty is truth and truth is beauty'. 'Satyam, Shivam, Sunderam' 'Satyam Gyanam Anantam Brahma'. (Absolute wisdom is prevalent in eternity and in the silent and vibrant universe). We are to go beyond our minds. Truth itself is an experience of existentialism. There is nothing 'Satan' by name in the total creation. 'Srineventa biswe amritasya putra'. It was stated by the Great Upanishads "Mankind of the world! Listen! You are the offspring of the most powerful nectarine universe," you are in it and it is in you. If our consciousness grows and reaches the top, we are blessed to do the supreme work. We are just like waves in the ocean. Sometimes we are here in the ocean and sometimes disappear but the ocean continues to be the same endless one.

When Jesus Christ was asked by his disciples about the kingdom of God he replied, "There will be time no longer." Please don't get flabbergasted and frustrated for 'Nothingness'. It is the greatest source of life, the greatest light, the greatest enlightenment, the greatest 'nothingness'. I started meditating in jail. I asked Mukhtar bhai to get me a copy of holy Koran too. PB Shelley, in his famous poem 'To a Skylark' wrote, "We look before and after and pine for what is naught/ our sincerest laughter with some pain is fraught/ our sweetest songs are those that tell of saddest thought." I agree with him in all respects. But is it true that our sweetest songs always tell of saddest thoughts. Life is a mystery, the more we know, the more we understand that life is an absolute mystery, an absolute joy. In his later poems 'Prometheus Unbound' Shelley was highly optimistic of Man and Life. For worldly hindrances and manmade problems, we are always afraid. None can give us security from outside. It always comes from the innermost soul. That is why poor, sick, ailing, and dying John Keats never felt insecure "A thing of beauty is joy forever" was felt by his very innermost soul. He did not find difference between Truth and Beauty. Absolute Truth is absolutely beautiful. Probably on the other hand Shelley was a bit confused, rich, handsome desperate and optimistic about total mankind. But he also had an accidental death in the Gulf of Spezia of Italy in his late twenties. I cannot make my journey to that absolute 'nothingness' like John Keats. So, I am afraid, unsafe and confused. I am afraid of death, afraid of my future life behind the bars.

My children, every day is your day, every morning is your morning, every week is your week, so are the months, the years, the decades, the epochs, the centuries, the millennia, even the eternity. As the 'New Men' you shall have to know depth of the sky, the power of the sun, power and beauty of the galaxies, the black holes, the universe, the eternity, the mother earth and her children from the universe. I can visualize those ensuing enlightened days of the world from my seclusion, even in the darkest night, in the darkest cell in my darkest physical trauma. From delight all beings are born, by delight we exist and grow, to that eternal delight we all go back. "Anandam, Anandam,

Anandam." Delight of being universal, delight for being eternal, delight for being a part of the eternity and eternal light. There is a delight, an ecstasy in our existence, existence of the Mother Earth, the Moon, the Sun, the galaxies, the universe, the omnipotent, the omniscient, the omnipresent Supreme Light. We all have emanated from that light. There is no difference between that greatest Jyoti(light) and us. We are from it and the light in 'ourselves', only for Maya we are not able to know the absolute beauty. This super hypnotism is allowing us to love and let love, hate and let hate.

Piramanayangam wrote to me and I was overjoyed. I used to call him 'Peera' when he was my student. He was shocked to know of my condition. Now at least I might get a chance to get myself acquitted to lead a free life, to race with my students and create a new world society, a war-free, violence free, exploitation free world society. A delightful society where lives are living in ecstasy and creativity. I described in writing my own life history to Mukhtar bhai. Told him how I became a convict and in the aftermath a Naxalite to our government. I opened my mind, my plan, my dreams, and my earnest desire to be free from this cursed and blessed life in jail. It is blessed for I came to rediscover myself in jail. I handed over that brief note secretly when he was on his regular rounds. In his congenial smile in the next meeting, I got a message of utmost cooperation from him for my acquittal.

My days began changing. A golden tinge of hope loomed large from behind the cluster of dark clouds. I am waiting and counting days for Piramanayangam. I applied to Mukhtar bhai, to allow me to write to Pira, but it was denied for one reason or the other. Both Mr Reddy and Ramaswamy were as good as Mukhtar bhai. But as I am a critical criminal in the hands of law, they could not help me much, even they could not change my cell. Finding no choice, during night, I began meditating, not for salvation but for achieving confidence, tolerance, and it was pleasant beyond description. In the Gita the reality in expressed in proper order "*Sambhabami yuge yuge,* " where that supreme power assures that he would reach the world in every age when necessity demands.

Children! Nothing is more mysterious and mystical than man and Man created the most beautiful one 'God'. Let us decide whether God created Man or Man created God. God and man are the counterpart of each other. Without the Supreme there could have been no Man, and without Man, Supreme world would have become most meaningless.

One evening Reddy came to me during my evening stroll, I was practically limping for severe pain in my legs. He caught hold of my right hand and said, "Masterji, Piramanayangam will reach you within a week." I was overjoyed by the news but did not express it outwardly. Secretly he thrust a small envelope in my uniform's pocket. I became much keen on getting to my cell to read it out for I was told that it was a letter from Peera. I opened up the envelope, it was a letter. It was from Piramanayangam. I read it in the weak light of my cell. It was not an emotional outpour as he had never been emotional. But he promised to meet me shortly.

I applied to Mukhtar Sahib to allow me to follow all formalities to prove my innocence. He met and we discussed many things but I forgot to remind him of my application. The next morning a warden came with two guards, opened the gate of my cell and commanded me to follow him to the main gate. I began walking with them through the brick built narrow road by the neglected lawn. I reached a corridor and was escorted to the office. Mukhtar sahib was sitting there along with three more officers. I was introduced by him to a lanky, smart, clean shaven IPS officer and he was Piramanyangam. Had I not been introduced I would have not recognized him.

From him I got to know of colleagues, who were no more in this mortal world -- Mala di died of cancer, my colleague for more than two decades, she was like my mother though she was elder to me by nine months only. Pira showed me the same respect as he did as a student, while talking he stood throughout. I told explicitly to him regarding my imprisonment. An hour later I was asked by Mukhtar bhai to return to my cell. Piramanyangam did not express his mind about me nor did I ask him to help me get out of jail, but felt very positive after meeting him.

Onwards, onwards, onwards and onwards! Earth is a small planet, like a speck of dust in the abysmal vastness of space. The universe is an unending desert. How can Earth be the only oasis? There may be extra-terrestrial civilizations. If all countries of the earth are not unified into a single world state or world federation, we shall soon become extinct. Apothecary of

UN has already been proved futile in the very beginning of this century. But I believe a 'New and Great age' will soon come. A definitive movement is in the offing. It must produce a great number of geniuses who are greater than the ones who had already appeared on the face of the earth in various spheres of life, an era of 'Galaxy of Talents.'

Meanwhile, a messenger from Piramanayangam came and asked me to apply to the authority to engage a lawyer. But who will finance me? I was told that a philanthropic organization in Chennai is ready to fight for me. I was overwhelmed. I came to know that Mrs Apparao is also collecting funds. Some of my students are well placed in USA and Europe and they got to know of my present condition. Sunny Bhownani, Aditya, Vijay, Parag, Debashish expressed their intention to stand by me, I was their English teacher since 1979. They loved me very much. I felt in the world movement I needed people like Pira and others.

Chapter 13
Freedom at Last

1

A lady lawyer arrived soon, brought by Urmila, Pira's wife. I was called to the jail office and introduced to Urmila and lawyer Sudha. Sudha discussed the case with me. They got some papers signed by me. I was meditating for two hours in my cell, and read some pages from the Holy Bible. In an article on Bible Sir David Attenborough writes: "the first words uttered by God in Genesis 1: 28 is Be fruitful and multiply, and fill the Earth and subdue it; and have dominion over the fish of the sea, and over the birds of the air, and over every living thing that moves upon the Earth." In a way Attenborough blames such attitude for Nature's destruction and adds: "Darwin's great insight revolutionized the way in which we see the world ...... Evolution is not just a theory, it is a historical fact, it is a science.

Mukhtar bhai sent his emissary to me. I was informed that court preparation for my freedom was on. A few days ago, Sudha, my generous lawyer was served a notice by the court to place me before 'My Lord'. One forenoon I was bedecked by the police with hand cuffs and taken to the court room. The judge was in his early forties, lawyers were moving around, wires of the ceiling fans were hanging like veins of a dissected dead body, I was thirsty and nervous. Sudha asked me to take a seat realizing my condition. I tried to sit but was dashed by the *peshkar* with ferocity. I fell down. I was a criminal and I was not supposed to be seated. I felt insulted, felt like crying, but instantly I was warned that I would be on my knees if I try to sit again.

The judge measured me as if I would soon be butchered. After some time, Sudha asked me to go outside. Our work with the court was over for that day. We came out and she whispered: "Sorry Sir, most of our courts are like this." She did not know that I saw our courts innumerable times before I became a Principal. In sweltering heat, they are donning black coats, high collar, white trousers and shoes which were sometimes cheap and mended, sometimes costly as per their practice and fame. Still judges are addressed 'My Lord' and they flaunt with pride and bravado. The switch of colonialism is very much incandescent in our courts.

The process of my release from jail was traumatizing for me. I kept writing to my students to forget this trauma. I have become eager to see the world beyond the jail walls. A couple of weeks elapsed but no real hope loomed, everything is entirely up to our judicial system. Whom should I blame? I enjoy plunging into my writing to the future citizens of the world.

Do you know on the 28th of March, 2009 billions of people across the world had their lights switched off for an hour with a view to emphasizing the urgent need for action on Global Warming for securing a bright future for mankind? Every citizen and every person of the world must pledge unanimously to conserve energy and to give checkmate to Global Warming. Barrack Obama said in Prague that the goal of ridding the world of its nuclear arsenal will not be reached perhaps in his life time. 'The Carnegie Endowments International Non- Proliferation Conference' is held in Washington every two years. Global disarmament organizations are less competent than Rotary International or Lion's Club. The Earth today is as helpless like my languishing mother in multifarious maladies before she died. No one thinks of the ill effects of climate change.

2

50,000 years ago, Man or Homo sapiens were created. But we are unable to utilize technology, astronomy and achievements of science for the welfare of mankind. In the unified world we shall be able to build a solar power station in the space and we shall be able to utilize 98% of solar energy. We shall have 60 times more energy in the earth. If we had a unified world government, we could avoid nuclear disasters like we had in Chernobyl or even nuclear warfare. We must expand ourselves into the space. We will be able to build miniature worlds for our accommodation. America was unknown to the Europeans, but after discovery of Christopher Columbus they plunged into the New Continent. In 1607 it was a barren land. Ultimately America surpassed

European countries. Miniature world shall have to be accepted by us for better tomorrows. The world governments spend 500 billion dollars every day for so called defense. Why not use this money for improvement of human lives?

In our new world government, one must be able to think and do better to solve our personal and national problems. Everybody must think for the world, dream of the world, work for the world. They shall serve Mother Earth and her best children, Homo sapiens. Only in the unification of the world and setting up of the World Government, Homo sapiens shall be able to salvage their 50,000 old civilizations. Thus they will be able to survive in the world till the last date of Mother Earth's life, definitely with comfort, creativity, dream, love and progress without militarism, warfare, terrorism, sectarianism, chauvinism, fanaticism, infection, diseases, child death and malnutrition. My aspiration, my passion and dream --- to make you all a part of that great movement of the millennium. In our beautiful planet which country is run without lie? Democracy and elections of most of the countries stand on vilification and mudslinging. Most ridiculous scenario is Bill Clinton's impeachment in a country like the United States of America, where freedom of man in all dimensions is the best. In so called modern times of the world of politics, Churchill, Nasser, Tito, Indira Gandhi, Mao dze dong, Stalin, Khrushchev and many other mediocre leaders like them were patriots. Leaders like Marx, Gandhi, Roosevelt, Kennedy, Martin Luther King (Jr), Nelson Mandela are internationalists, lovers of the Homo sapiens, lovers of our most beautiful planet in the universe. Barack Obama said to the Americans, "We are the people, we have been waiting." But a single nation's rising in materialistic world shall never help mankind's real awakening and emancipation from odds. I would rather say, you are the students of the world, are the people for whom the world has been waiting for thousands of years, let us give salutations to the Neanderthals, for they are your ancestors, my ancestors, our ancestors.

Peace shall never come from classroom's teaching as morality can never be taught by teaching moral science in schools. It is a historical necessity and an integral part of human evolution. And 'now is the time'. If environmental pollution and partial catastrophe be vibrant like militarism, terrorism, deadly diseases and corruption, after certain time the opposite must also happen. It already reached the zenith by the dictation of time and it shall gradually come downwards to reach its Nadir. And the interim vacuum shall be filled in by peace, spiritual awakening, and awareness of every kind, love, world unification, progress in every dimension, creativity and creation. Super soul of creation exists in an absolute domain outside our time and space. When things are unbridled, they get destroyed after certain period. Evil of every soul run amuck aimlessly and it must fall shortly. Unbridled capitalism brought about a tremendous economic meltdown as unbridled Sovietism did. It collapsed. Collapse of the Soviet is not an end but a beginning of a journey to discover new horizon. Neither reinless Marxism nor reckless capitalism shall dawn a new era. Like Sovietism, ultra-capitalism shall collapse giving rise to spiritualism. Super spiritual awakening and awareness is an integral and quintessential part of evolution and progress of history of man. Ultimate power rests in you and deep rooted in the very core of your mind, heart and beyond. Students of the world Know thyself 'Atmanam biddhi' (Know your soul) 'Aham brahmas mi'(I am He, I am Eternity). You, you and only you are the creators for an outstanding phenomenal era for the universe, nature, the Mother Earth and the almighty. The universe is God, the mankind, and the representatives from the eternity are prophets. We are created by the omnipotent eternity to know it, to substantiate it. There is an evolutionary impulse in the universe and we the mankind had that legacy from our super ancestors, the universe. You are the universe; we are the universe. The earth, the sun, the stars, galaxies, blackholes are the members of the universe, as we are. No fear. Onwards, onwards, onwards.

These days, democracy and elections of most countries stand on vilification and mudslinging. Remember Bill Clinton's impeachment in a country like the United States of America, where freedom of man in all dimensions is considered supreme? Barack Obama said to the Americans, "We are the people, we have been waiting." But a single nation's rising in materialistic world shall never help mankind's real awakening. Peace shall never come from classroom teaching, as morality can never be taught. It is a historical necessity and an integral part of human evolution. And 'now is the time.'

My children! Remember this poor mother Earth is the richest temple of living God, which is man.

Eternity, the *mahakala*, synchronized the frenzied spiritual system and that synchronization is God the almighty. Norman Borlaug, the greatest hunger fighter of all time, fifty percent of the world population is able to go to bed at night after having food only for this great philanthropic scientist. His research improved wheat varieties and led to the Green Revolution. Such people are not seen on history pages, rather we find emperors, kings, warriors, mass killers. Knowing the Absolute Truth Buddha attained *nirvana*. Jesus sacrificed his life; Muhammad dedicated himself for the cause of the poor tribals of Arabia. Albert Einstein got surprised and accepted the philosophy of Spinoza after a phenomenal and great discovery. The absolute truth remains undiscovered. Corruption can destroy even the best discovery of men. Kill corruption and save Man. "Truth and non-violence are as old as the hills," said Gandhi. But lies and violence are younger …. And they rule. So many warmongers were selected for Nobel prize, yet those like F.D. Roosevelt and Gandhi were denied. In recent times, the Chinese government shall be one of the greatest stumbling blocks for unification of the world. Chairman Mao of China wrote in his Red book, "Masses are the greatest heroes." And during Deng's governance thousands of students were gunned down and bulldozed in Tiananmen Square for they were worshippers of democracy.

Piramanayangam came last evening. He embraced me, sobbed for he was officially informed by the Home Ministry that I was a terrorist. He advised me to write to the President of India, assuring me he would fight for me and added he would consult Mrs Ranjita Apparao, one of the most outstanding lawyers in the High Court of Chennai. I asked Pira to get a letter prepared for the President drafted by Mrs Apparao or any other lawyer of that stature. In our country there is a judicial gridlock. It is neither transparent nor secret. It is still functioning for good number of outstanding lawyers and some best men of the countries who are judges in the High Court and apex Courts. But criticism may lead to contempt of court.

I wrote a few lines to Mrs Apparao referring to our friendship in Raipur during early seventies and handed it over to Pira. I did not talk to anybody for two consecutive days. On the third day Pira sent Urmila to get some dummy papers signed by me. Soon I got to know that Mrs Apparao is creating a fund to free me and many others languishing in jail. There were many like Dr Binayak Sen, Praful Jha in Chhattisgarh, Lachit Bordoloi in Assam, Herman Gonsalves in Nasik, Arun Ferreira, Ashok Reddy, Dhanendra Bhurula, Naresh Bansode in Vidarbha, Prashant Rahi in Uttarakhand, Pittala in Sri Sailem in Andhra Pradesh, arrested under UAPA for alleged Maoist links and in jail. I felt proud of being enlisted with all these great people fighting for Human Rights and for the poor. But I could not serve men with utmost devotion and dedication like them. Apparao expressed her heartfelt sympathy for me. She promised to join our crusade after my release but advised me to think over the downtrodden plight of innumerable sufferers in the remote corners of our country's villages and that of the world. Without their welfare no welfare work shall be tangible. Many Gandhians were working for welfare, education and healthcare of Gonds, Koyas and Murias, the *adivasis*. Since I was brought up at Pakhanjore in Chhattisgarh and erstwhile Madhya Pradesh, I was only accustomed to incompetent bureaucratic system of Dandakaranya Refugee Project. Nobody was concerned with the *adivasis*. I had no feelings for those half naked innocent aborigines who spent their lives with boiled rice and *fullies* (local alcohol). Even none around me had any empathy for them. I only once enjoyed a drama *'Chandeli Gonda'* at Bhanupratappur during my night halt on my way to Raipur, probably in August 1974. Whereas Dr Sen plunged into their service with his wife, Mrs Ilina Sen. Vinayak Sen said, "It's a Kafkaesque world in the jail of Chhattisgarh. There is no human dignity..."

3

Meanwhile, Urmila brought Mrs Apparao who came to meet me in jail. They got enthused to free me after exoneration of Dr Binayak Sen. I caught hold of Mrs Apparao's hands in excitement and she assured me she would shortly work with me on my ideas of world freedom and unification. She would soon come to meet me again with all legal papers and a robust legal practitioner of South India. I was highly optimistic. I was informed that I might be served a notice by the court of this state by the dint of the efforts of Pira, Sudha, Mrs Apparao, Dr Manipadam, Justice Mohan, ex-judge of the Supreme Court of India, are supreme men. A great philanthropic organization of

South India patronized to grant my bail. Gradually my meal in the jail began improving. Still, I was not allowed to write letter to any. My advocates were working tremendously to prove that I was not Sataroop Goswamy, a Naxalite leader, as I was mistaken for him. They now had to prove my identity as a School Principal from Kolkata. I was informed that Greta mothered a baby boy a couple of months ago. But still she or anyone from my family did not know my whereabouts and whether I was alive. Probably none guessed I was languishing in jail in a remote corner of South India.

One fine November evening, I was informed by the jail Super that some important plenipotentiary had come to meet me. Piram, Urmila and Sudha came with Aditya Banerjee, my closest student and ICSE candidate of 1984. He is a big shot now staying in Sweden. He embraced me. Aditya was keen for bailing me out. He told me that he had married a Swedish girl and was running a big business of international order. I was given many legal papers to sign. Aditya handed me over a packet of South Indian sweetmeats, and the Gita translated into English by Dr Sarvapalli Radha Krishnan. Mukhtar bhai my jail super allowed me to have them. Aditya's arrival with Pira, Urmila and Sudha was a cathartic experience for me. I believe in destiny and '*karma*' Only destiny is the infallible one. Swami Vivekananda said, "Thus, day by day Karma's powers spent release the soul forever...... Nor I, nor thou, nor God nor man. The 'I' has all become, The all is 'I' and bliss. Om tat sat, Om."

"......from bonds, be free!
Be not afraid. This mystery, My shadow,
cannot frighten me!
Know once for all that I am He!"
he again sermonized,

"The knowledge of Brahman (universe, cosmic power) is the ultimate goal – the highest destiny of man. But man cannot remain absorbed in Brahman all the Time! When he comes out of it, he must have something to engage himself. At that time, he should do such work as well contribute real well-being of people. Therefore, I do urge you in the service of *Jiva*s in a spirit of oneness."

Sudha and Aditya came with Mr G Nagarajan, a reputed lawyer. Very likely he is a bar-at-law. I learnt from him that real Satarup Goswamy has not yet been found, and the government was hence delaying my bailing out thinking I was either that man or had links with him. I have got jinxed, "Justice delayed means justice denied."

Chapter 14
Fighting with Cancer

1

Three days later, I was informed I would be taken to the criminal court and might get bail. I got myself shaven, had a proper haircut and got dressed as per Aditya and Pira's plans. I was escorted to the office of Mukhtar Bhai. Pira, Aditya, Urmila received me and boarded their car and I climbed into the police jeep. I am flying towards my freedom. My friends in their car were waiting for me at the court gate. There were photographers around, was I being thronged as Satarup Goswamy?

My lawyers Sudha and Nagarajan were in a black lawyer's gown. I could not make out anything about their conversation with the judge. He seemed to be young and handsome. Most part of the altercation and conversation was going on in South Indian language. At last, I was given bail! It was a surprise. My comrades accompanied me outside with dignity and silence. But people outside were uproarious on seeing me. Probably for them I was still be Satarup Goswamy.

After my release, Pira and Aditya booked a hotel in the neighbouring town. Mukhtar bhai told me that he would visit me and hugged and Aditya was holding my hands. After reaching the hotel gate I was attacked by journalists once again. Pira and Aditya tried to do everything incognito. I failed to sleep that night. Ultimately at 7am, Aditya's melodious rendering of Tagore's song helped me to leave my bed. It was a new life now, as if I was from an alien's world, I had got so acclimatized to jail life. Was it really a freedom? In the car Aditya broke the non-plussed silence. Probably we all were dumbfounded with my dramatic freedom. Aditya began singing a Tagore song in Bengali-*"eki labanye punno prana pranesha he/ ananda basanta samagame..."* The sky was overcast with dark clouds the wind was blowing; white birds were flying in the sky. Then suddenly the rain fell.

We all decided to take a night halt in the nearest town. The downpour continued incessantly. Aditya said, "Sir, in our school days you used to say that Liberation always comes from the barrel of guns. Why did you say that when today you are against violence?"

"It is the quotation of chairman Mao of China. And today I believe gun does not kill man, only man kills man. Peace does not come from Heaven, it comes from man. Hell does not export violence; it lives inside us as does dormant goodness and God." All on a sudden I went back to the early eighties. Both Aditya and Pira were in 9th standard. "Still I am unable to free myself totally from violence and malice. It is the toughest job of the world," said I. "We are always responsible for our own mess. Non-violence, proper and correct understanding, and love are historical necessity for man. If within a few decades we fail to change our total mindset, our existence shall be in jeopardy.

By 2050 world population shall reach nine billion. In spite of our excellent scientific and technological progress if we cannot grow food grains for all, we shall die of hunger, world unification is essential. It must change the process and way of politics, politicians, and political institutions randomly. Global mal distribution, poverty, pigmy politicians, and dwarfed bureaucrats of today are failing to keep pace with rapid progress of science and time. With rapid development of science and technology men try to keep that speed of mind.

Aditya said, "But war is also inevitable with progress of science and technology." I could not control myself and shouted, "War, war, war and war. Don't you think your own child can also be killed in war! We destroy through science and enjoy destruction subconsciously. Every country of the world is victimized by a monolithic virus of psychological disorder. Look at the Ethiopians, famished in hunger, ninety five percent of their money exhausted for buying lethal weapons surreptitiously. It is a clandestine business open to all. The world needs a marvelous group of powerful psychoanalysts."

Pira was our guide. He decided a night halt at the nearest town in a Government rest house. I tried to relax in the car. Pira told we might continue our journey for more than two hours. Sudha suggested that we might make a night halt at Elluru. All agreed including the driver. That day I got the news about Dantewada's massacre of 76 CRPF by the Maoists. They were camping in Tarmetila jungle of Chhattisgarh. Again a massacre!! The jungles of Dandakaranya is full of Maoists. My father made forecast decades ago during his stay. He said, "There may be a tremendous sanguinary movement in the Dandakaranya for total negligence of the Government of India and government of the state."

DNK project was introduced for the displaced people of the then erstwhile East Pakistan. But no governmental measure was taken for the tribal people who lived there. Seldom had any minister gone there for a visit apart from Jay Sukhlal Hathi and Dr Manmohan Das. Dr Das was the Chairman of the project and Deputy Rehabilitation Minister. Most of the tribals saw tube well after our arrival and arrival of the refugees. During the span of Arvind Netam, the then member of parliament from Kanker some fragmented problems of the *adivasis* were_brought to the forefront. He was a minister and also paid visits. In DNK's Parlakote zone, Himangshu Dutta Majumder was the zonal and tribal administrator. He and his officials did not try to do anything for the tribes. They occupied the *adivasi*'s land in lieu of meager amount and bottles of *phully*, local alcoholic drink from *mohua*. Black market rackets were predominant for *tendu pattas*, and it is still going on. After Bhanu Pratappur, till late eighties, there were no schools for the *adivasi* children. Schools in Chhotta Kapsi and Pakhanjore were opened for refugee children and children of the project employees. My father was the Headmaster of Chhotta Kapsi School.

Even in Pakhanjore High School, there was not a single *adivasi* child. Most tehsildars were incompetent, neither the government of independent India nor the state governance had time to pay attention to them. During my school days in Chhattisgarh, Dandakaranya, seldom politicians from Raipur or Durg visited our place. Census was not done. Election of 1966 was an election of farce. There was not a single *adivasi* voter and 75% Bengalis along with my father could not cast vote for their names were not in the voter list.

Jaisukhlal Hathi was given a Viceroy's welcome in Pakhanjore, Kapsi and Khayerkatta in 1966. Maoist Movement was made a phenomenon likewise. By ravaging the Maoist no solution can be worked out. Naxalites were killed ruthlessly in West Bengal in 1972-73 but they awoke again in the outskirts of West Bengal, Jharkand, Andhra's border and Chhattisgarh. Who are responsible for this? We all are responsible. We enjoy films with violence. We buy our children toy weapons to play with; we nurture naked patriotism and fundamentalism. In our global villages we need people like Sunderlal Bahuguna, a noted environmentalist and follower of Gandhi, Wangeri Mathai, founder of Green Belts Movement.

Night hung upon me, upon the hotel, upon Eluru. Again, there was a mysterious silence all around like the prison. Probably Aditya, Pira and Urmila were very tired. Next morning after having tea, I bathed and readied for the ferry to Chennai. Our car jolted as we entered Tamil Nadu. Pira told me many of his classmates, my students were waiting in Chennai to receive me.

En route we stopped for tea where I befriended two French devotees of Rishi Aurobindo and Sri Ma. One was a lecturer in a university, a member of the French Communist Party. His father was an industrialist. He left everything and joined the global spiritual movement of Sri Aurobindo like thousands of others from France. He believed that in our times there were two lovers and unifiers of mankind. Marx and Aurobindo. According to him both were saints. The former chalked out programme and project for World Unification. The viceroy of the proletariats. His slogan is "proletariats of the world unite!" Aurobindo irradiated the principle of super evolution for unique unification of Man.

I finally halted at Uthukottai, Aditya extended his leave. Rahul Mukherjee and Subhasish Banerjee came to stay with me along with Lekhu. They were batch mates, had passed the ICSE Examination in 1984. New dresses were tailored for me.

2

My stay at Eluru was one of the happiest episodes of my life. I was not allowed to go beyond the periphery of the bungalow. All four of us strolled in the garden. I spent moonlit nights with my students even though they were all adults now, they hurled questions and I answered like I did in their school days. Lekhu was from USA, Rahul from Russia, Aditya from Sweden and Subhasish from Calcutta. We discussed Vedas, Upanishads, anarchism, Buddha, Marxism, Roosevelt, Gandhi, Sartre,

Vivekananda, Tagore, many doctrines, principles and many such things along with the revolt of Islam, Jesus, and Sufis. We travelled together to Avalon, the place of the blessed where heroes enjoy life after death according to Celtic mythology. All along we were talking, laughing, singing, clapping and discussing. Our vehicle was an image of the mighty world.

Rahul was always dexterous in concocting a cock and bull story like he had shaken hands with George Bush Sr, when he had worked as a waiter in Moscow. I wished my journey should never end. "We rode it seemed my spirit flew"— Probably and most probably it was my last joy, in my 'Camelot'. We were nearing Chennai. The light of the moonlit night was receding and incandescent electric lights were gradually becoming omnipresent. Artificial light extinguished our enlightened joy. Pira's car was guiding us. From our car, I saw IPS Piramanyangam was on his cell phone. Both the cars had a left-hand turn, entered through a big gate and stopped in front of a posh hotel, Raintree, Annasalai.

I was welcomed by Dr J Manipadam and Mr Balan. I had come to Chennai many times, most of them were known to me, Mrs Apparao came with a large bouquet of flowers. Getting them all together, I was in tears. I was given a big room with three beds. Dr Manipadam and Mrs Apparao chatted for a short while with me. They were upset about the Bhopal Gas Tragedy on December 5, 1984. They had come back from Bhopal the previous day with their team. They expressed how the clerics of gas tragedy escaped even 26 years after. They wanted to go to court for my preposterous imprisonment and harassment. But I know that effort would also be preposterous. I requested them to pay attention to Bhopal Gas Tragedy for financial aid, medical rehabilitation and environmental remedy. The main miscreant Warren Anderson's extradition from USA is also question like a bone of contention. He was the chairman of Union Carbide at the time of world's worst industrial accident.

We planned to go to Tirupathi, but as I was getting ready, I felt excruciating pain in my abdomen and I was whisked off to Apollo Hospital. Dr Tyagarajan checked me and diagnosed a urinary tract infection. I was advised immediate hospitalization. All my tests were done and the diagnosis was prostate cancer, metastasis has set in full swing and immediate operation was necessary. I was urinating blood. The cost of my operation was borne by my students. After operation, my chemotherapy would start, in the first phase six chemos would be given. I only hoped that I would get OK and travel back to Calcutta to meet my students, my family and Greta. The pain was so unbearable at a point that I became unconscious.

Lying on the hospital bed staring at a bleak future, I kept thinking of who funded the mammoth revolutions like the one I wished to launch. I have no idea who financed the French Revolution. Russian revolution was allegedly financed by rich bankers like Paul Warburg, Rockefeller, Morgan Rothschild. The Russian Czars were anti Jews and in protocols of the elders of Zion, a Zionists conference monitored by the powerful Jews for dominating the world power in 1897 in Switzerland. Many pundits stated that this protocol of the Zion was a forgery. Powerful domineering Zionists financed Russian Revolution. It is said most of the Bolshevik stalwarts were Jews apart from Lenin and Stalin. Even Krupskaya, Lenin's wife was of Jew descent. Revolution of China was financed by the Soviet Russia. In today's world there are many super rich juggernauts who are philanthropists and world society reformers. They shall be our greatest financial pillars.

Reaction of chemotherapy was hazardous and traumatic. My hair began falling like dry leaves. One night I was frightened, looking at myself on a wall mirror. I was continuously vomiting. I had severe stomach upset. I got severely emaciated. Now I cannot work without help. If I die, I will try to die not with trauma but with joy and dignity. Death is the most important part of our entire life. It is a fulfillment and culmination of every life. Mother Earth was once born. The sun, the moon, the galaxies, the black holes, the supernova including our milky way were born. The Big Bang is their parents, our parents. So, we shall all die. Our solar family shall die too someday, only power and force shall never die. Stephen Hawking in his last book 'The Grand Design' co-authored with Leonard Mlodinow states, "Because there is a law such as gravity, the universe will create itself from Nothing. Spontaneous creation is the reason there is something rather than nothing, why the universe exists." Thus, nothing is everything. The greatest zero is the great energy, greatest intelligence, greatest consciousness. In fact, that 'Something' is Almighty, that super power, super consciousness, supramental force. Cosmic power is God. I am trying to discover the riddle of death from my cancer bed. Really every life is a grand design including the entire universe, the solar system, the Mother Earth, birth and death too.

I want to come back to our planet over and over again. Mother Earth is the most beautiful lady of the universe. If really there is a way to return to her! One morning the doctor consented that I can finally travel back to Kolkata. As I was recovering, my hair was growing back. I came back to the hotel from the hospital. Debashish Mantri, my ex-student of 1984 accompanied me.

What should I do in my dying condition after my return! My students will keep me alive. I feel like joining all the movements of the world for human rights, freedom and democracy with teenagers who always act bravely to change India's media and politicians. Only right guidance is needed.

3

Masses of the world are more alert than before and everyone wishes for a democracy. You must mark uprising in Egypt, Tunisia, Syria, Bahrain, Libya, Yemen and many other countries in Arab world. Sectarian problem and the problems of ethnicity in these places are the greatest stumbling blocks. Talibans are creation of the government of USA in 80's. It was accentuated during the regime of Carter, Reagan and George Bush (Sr). Afghanistan was a playing field of Imperial British and Tsarist Russia. After the collapse of Soviet in the period of Mikhail Gorbachev, fanatic Afghanistan became the playing field of the government USA and the militant insurgents. Unfortunately, 9/11 was the nemesis for the innocent citizens of the USA. Theocrats of Pakistan may be the greatest stumbling blocks in this ensuing Global Revolution. Pakistan once gave this world one of the most peace-loving giants, Khan Abdul Ghaffar Khan or Frontier Gandhi. From 1979 fundamental *mujahid*s were trained by USA government on the soil of Pakistan for more than a decade to foil the USSR encroachment of Afghanistan. What a pathetic condition both Afghanistan and Pakistan are facing now.

During World War I, Tagore wrote, "It is the National and Commercial egoism, which is the evil harbinger of war…." He again wrote, "The demon of barbarity has given up all pretense and has emerged with unconcealed fangs, ready to tear up humanity in an orgy of devastation. From one end of the world to the other poisonous fumes of hatred darken the atmosphere. And yet I shall not commit the grievous sin of losing faith in man. I would rather look forward to the opening of a new chapter." I too dream of such a world.

Your generation is endowed with information, communication, and science and apex technology. You are well aware of quintessence of environment, the earth, the sun, the universe and mammoth powerful nature. Environment is being destroyed at a fast pace, Russia is burning with wildfires, Leh a snow desert experienced a tremendous cloudburst, Pakistan has been ravaged and ransacked by a diabolic flood, in Greenland a huge iceberg broke, four times the size of Manhattan. Who is responsible?

I came to know from Aditya that Tamosha had settled with a Jew writer in Mumbai and my son is practicing law in Mumbai High Court but there was no news of Greta. Meanwhile, Egypt's military administration allowed the countrymen to go for democracy. Gradually democracy will inundate all countries and may be one day we shall have a single World Democracy. Change is a mobile process. Change is joy. Wars and natural disaster spoiled many great creations of man along with mammoth library of Alexandria. Wars are the worst discoveries of man that thrived, a sport of killings, Olympics of genocide. It is sheer savagery. The greatest light is awaiting man.

July 4, 2012 was a great day for humanity as CERN scientists discovered God Particle. Though the Bose Einstein statistics and Bose Einstein Condensate Theory was not nominated for Nobel Prize, Subatomic particle Boson was named by Einstein in 1920. For Prof Satyendra Nath Bose guessed existence of that phenomenal subatomic particle. Scientist Peter Higgs began their universal quest in 1964. Higgs Boson is responsible for lending mass to the particles and formed stars and planets, sun, moon, and our home Earth. It was all created 13.7 billion years ago. It is really a giant leap not only for CERN, scientists and for the West but it is a colossal stride for mankind.

I have been shifted from Hotel Raintree to Dr Manipadam's house. It is quite comfortable, Aditya and Debashish Mantry returned home, my health condition is somewhat well but I am not free from cancer. I told Dr Manipadam and Madam Apparao to arrange everything for me to go to Calcutta before my condition worsens any further. In Dr Manipadam's house I am at present looked after by his daughter-in-law. Both Mrs Manipadam and her daughter-in-law are wonderful ladies. Their affection is beyond measure. We have got to reach the masses of the world to let them understand the benefit of world unification. Definitely not under any particular national umbrella.

In our planet, millions of powerful species are born. Their physical conditions are amenable to Nature. Physically these kindred were powerful enough to fight Nature. Homo sapiens are the weakest physical creatures and they rule the planet. Every street dog is far stronger physically than a single man. Then how are we ruling the world? It is only because of our intelligence and rationality. But I envisage a world where there will be no killing, no murder, and no rape. There will be no mafia, no greed, no corruption, no dirty politicians, no violence, no war, and no death penalty.

Lev Tolstoy was an atheist, in his middle age he felt the veracity that life is not eternal. He was afraid of death like all of us. He resorted to pure Christianity with minimum faith in rituals and rites of the church. He was greatly inspired by 'Raj Yoga' of Swami Vivekananda. He authored three great novels along with innumerable short stories. His epoch-making novels are 'Anna Karenina', 'War and Peace' and 'Resurrection'. His 'Resurrection' is full of indirect references of Swami Vivekananda's 'Raj Yoga'. It stated about preposterousness of church and religious organizations. Swami Vivekananda was torchbearer and Tolstoy possessed a splinter of that light to guide man. That staunch atheists ultimately became a saint and renounced everything, neglected his family and left home in a wintry night for liberation of his soul, had respite in a station master's cabin and breathed his last. He was no longer afraid of his own death and his last words were "I want emancipation. I want emancipation". The Mahatma was much inspired by Tolstoy. He established 'Tolstoy Farm' with Mr Kallenbach in South Africa. Indirectly Swami Vivekananda was the real inspiration for both Tolstoy and Gandhi.

Once I wrote a letter to Malala Yousafzai, the 14-year-old girl who was shot by the Taliban on October 9, 2012. She was fighting for education of girl child in Pakistan. She was going back home from her school in a bus. Taliban gunmen stopped the bus and shot her in her head. Two more students Shazia Ramzan and Kainat Ahmed were also injured. She was transported to England for treatment. Surgeons of Pakistan had already removed one bullet. At Birmingham in England, she had an operation for more than 5 hours. Malala Yousafzai's valued life was saved. This girl told, "I don't mind if I have to sit on the floor of the school. All I want is education. And I am afraid of no one."

I wrote a letter to her:

Malala, my courageous daughter,

I am extremely proud of you. The world needs you. The ensuing movement of the world needs you. All the students, youth and children need you. I have a craving for decades to get innumerable daughters like you, who are imbibed with indomitable courage. Great gathering in Tahrir Square of Egypt and conglomeration of youths after Delhi rape case proved to a great extent that man can do everything. Youth of today are the light of our civilization in the near future. Till date our civilization is nothing but tombs of empires.

My child Malala, my mother was like you. You must be able to create storm as you did in Swat valley. Your sacrifice is not an end but a breakthrough. Hats off to your campaign for girls' education and promotion of secularism for which you were shot by the savages. My child! If I survive for a decade, I will meet you to be more inspired by your great self. I don't know if my letter will reach you. But my blessings always are there with you.

'*Charaibeti*'—Go ahead and go up.

There are millions of Malala Yousafzai in the world and billions are yet to be born. It is summer time. Chennai's heat is scorching and sweltering. I was taken to my oncologist for checkup. He gave a clearance certificate. Very recently I am enthused by a book, Globish (How the English language became the World's Language" authored by Robert McCurn. It is stated by a critic, "While the global dominance of Anglo-American power appears to be on the wane, the English language has acquired an astonishing new life of its own. With a supernational momentum, it is now able to zoom across time and space at previously unimaginable speed. In McCurn's analysis, the cultural revolution of our time is the emergence of English, a global phenomenon as never before, to become the world's language." In the 21st century, writes the author, 'English + Microsoft = Globish.'

Malala had said, "They thought (Taliban) that the bullets would silence us, but they failed. Out of that silence came thousands of voices. The terrorists thought that they would change our aims and stop our ambitions but nothing changed in my life except this; Weakness, fear, hopelessness died. Strength, courage, and power were born. I am the same Malala. My ambitions are the same. My hopes are the same. My dreams are the same." She is the youngest nominee in the history of Nobel Peace Prize. After a long time, Nobel Peace Prize will be sanctified if she is really awarded the prize. Millions of Malalas are latent in our world society. If Malala had been killed by the foolhardy Talibans, millions and millions shall expedite their arrival from the background where they are hidden by the system. Malalas are going to dawn a new epoch in this century. I am envious of her. She is great. She told, "We need peace for education." Absolutely correct. And I dare say, we need education for peace.

Super state concept is rampant in my optimistic dreams. One may think I am a dreamer, a Utopian. Dream gave birth to liberal cyber democracy. I am afraid; postmodern global market economy may shape neo-colonialism or postmodern hegemony. In that race again some country or countries may become economic super power to rule other nations. And greedy business tycoons may exploit poor nations. You, the young citizens of the world have got to be supremely and immaculately alert, awake and conscious against the bad storm of Global Market Economy, lest it might harm the world more than atomic war.

Chapter 15
Towards the Incarceration Again

1

I am increasingly reaching the end of my writing and my life. I was born probably with too big an ambition. I was ambitious to teach the stars and universe along with the black holes. Only the universe was my competitor. I felt like running the entire universe. But after a certain period of my life, I diverted my love for the universe to love for my Mother Earth.

In my childhood I was afraid of the reflection of the sun while bathing in our pond in erstwhile East Pakistan. Sometimes I used to go astray seeing my own reflection in the mirror. This feeling worsened when I joined a group of young school students at Kapsi, Bastar to cremate the dead body of a helpless peon's wife. She was consigned to the flames. I knew her quite well. I could not sleep nights together and began disliking my own body.

One of the most prolific English writers of India, Khushwant Singh wrote memoir. To make life meaningful, he in his book suggested not pondering over our arrival, our source, meaning of life, eternity of soul etc. According to him we must think and work seriously leaving all contemplation aside. But really, I beg to defer, for extraordinary thoughts on universe, eternity, evolution, source of life in the world, its value always attract me. The great eternity created extraordinary prophets, extraordinary thinkers, authors, poets, artists and extraordinary scientists, and for them only Mankind is able to survive along with our planet. Without them the entire world would have become a world of philanderers and barbarians.

2

Children, I met five wonderful lady teachers from the United States of America. They were dreamers. They came to Calcutta in teacher exchange programme for a month and were in

Chennai. Dr Manipadam brought them to me. United States India Educational Foundation conducts it every year. All were wearing sari, incidentally one of them, Jodi, was doing a project in my school in Calcutta. She taught English. She seemed to be a hard-working smart teacher and so was everybody. There was another called Sarah and Alexius. Caitlin came from the US as team leader. She was receptive, reserved and sober. Jodi is flamboyant, frank and talkative. 'Sarah the Great' is the greatest giggler of the world! Almost so was Alexius. But I am afraid 'Sarah the Wonderful' was a bit serious with me. I did not tell them that I am dying and was a carcinoma patient.

I told them, "We are under the same sun, same moon. Our stars are same and so are our planets. Even our race is same. We all belong to human race." They did not only accept but applauded and extolled.

Jodi being the English teacher discussed with me about Robert Frost, Walt Whitman, TS Eliot and his world famous "The Wasteland". I categorically referred to her the last lines of the poem quoted by TS Eliot from 'Brihad Aranyak Upanishad' and it is in Sanskrit. No. We did not finish everything in a day. On their way back to the United States they reached Chennai and had several meetings with me in the hotel along with my bosom friend Dr J Manipadam. I addressed Jodi as 'my daughter.' They are much elder than Malala, and I discovered in them Malala in other dimensions. They are the generation of peace and they shall bring about a sea change on our planet. Jodi told me, "Sir, within a century atom bomb may be prepared in many college laboratories of the world. There shall be no change unless we change world culture and mindset of the people of our planet." American educated youths are much advanced in mindset. Decades ago, citizens of England and United States protested en masse on the eve of Saddam Hussein's war. We discussed about mankind, world civilization in evenings around a big hotel table.

Jodi being the guest teacher of my school in Calcutta became very close. She is a Roman Catholic Christian and a staunch follower of Mother Teresa. Most of my girls from America came to me either in sari or in *salwar kameez.* Caitlin's personality to some extent resembled my mother. It was Caitlin's second visit to India. She was very fond of 'chai'. Shall I ever travel with them to the USA? But, how can I? When even reaching Calcutta is difficult for me! In fact, the civilization of our planet needs innumerable human beings like them. Girls of the world should go ahead to bring change and unification of the world. My daughter Jodi accepted my paternal affection. Before their departure for the USA, Dr Manipadam and I arranged a small farewell party. Caitlin and Jodi sang together a Bengali song of Tagore, the one from Satyajit Ray's '*Charulata*.' Jodi presented me with a book of world-famous Nigerian writer Chinua Achebe -- 'The Education of a British Protected Child'. Nelson Mandela said, "The writer in whose company the prison walls fell down". This is a volume of autobiographical essays. She gave me an American card of David Hughes and wrote, "Thank you for allowing me to be a part of your life, and I hope that we can continue to work together.

Your daughter,

Jodi."

Powerful despotic governments always try to throttle common man's voice. But we need to break the hands that throttle us. Military regime of Egypt declared emergency and hundreds were killed. No power can suppress Egyptian spring time awakening. But it shall come over the tombs of innumerable martyrs. Violence is the darkest ghost. Now it is 3am. I have insomnia. I have exhausted every idea, dream, and opinion for you all. I am exhausted to get you rid of this lunatic civilization, insane and insipid governance. When I write to you, I am oblivious of my pain, trauma, malady, hunger and thirst.

I am not effusively fighting to save my life from scourge of cancer. But I am writing with downright emotion to save human race and our home the Mother Earth. I am writing to my students to make your life meaningful, our existence fruitful. I am writing to change man, to change us, to change our mindset, to change the world. I believe if we cannot bring change, within a century we will be extinguished and the earth will be a burning planet.

It was immaculately and expressly observed by my friend Charles Chaplin. In Nazi Germany patriotism turned to chauvinism and culminated into barbarous genocide. Charles Chaplin said in his book *My Autobiography*: "I dislike being told whom to kill and what to die for – and all in the name of patriotism.... the fact is I am not a patriot, not for moral or intellectual reasons alone, but because I have no feeling for it.

How can one tolerate patriotism when six million Jews were murdered in its name? Some might say it was in Germany; nevertheless, these murderous cells lie dormant in every nation. I cannot vociferate about national pride and from what I have observed that cells of Nazism, although dormant at the moment, can be activated very quickly in every century."

The word globalization is used for globalization of the markets of the world. Very likely this market economy and information revolution may add strength for global unification, though personally I am against shopkeepers' culture. The world was run by super powerful shopkeepers even before the Industrial Revolution. The communist movement in Russia was financed by the Rothschild and Rockefeller families of England. Not that they loved communism but for Jew pogrom and genocide by Tsar of Russia they supported the movement. In fact, Jews were ruthlessly massacred during the tenure of Tsar Nicholas II. Both these filthy rich families are Jews. During the rule of Tsar Nicholas II innumerable Russian Jews were massacred. Russian revolution was run by Bolsheviks and Mensheviks. The former was a Communist party and the most powerful anti-Tsar group to destroy the Tsar and Tsarism. They deliberately became financial patrons of proletariat revolution being die hard Jew capitalists of the super-rich club. The Bolshevik Revolution had financial patronization by richest business tycoons of New York and London. Both Lenin and Trotsky were financed before, during and after the revolution. Members of the super- rich club of the world must really learn to love mankind and our planet. But to do that they have to relinquish greed to do the most important work in the history of man.

Patriotism, ultra-patriotism, chauvinism, religious fanaticism gave birth to die hard terrorism. Human progress in reality is never possible if mankind is not unified and religious and state barriers are not removed. Every peace process is futile without change of our mindset. The term World Peace is one of the most ridiculous terminologies of human history for its never possible until we start a great peace war with non-violence. Real welfare for every nation is possible if the world is unified and mankind becomes ambitious enough for our multifarious progress in real sense of the term. Failing which high handedness of so-called powerful nations has to be tolerated by a major portion of humanity.

Pete Seeger, the prolific singer, outstanding composer, imaginative persona, born world citizen is far away. He is no more. I and We must believe like him,

We shall overcome, we shall overcome,
We shall overcome someday;
Oh, deep in my heart, I do believe,
We shall overcome someday.

In 1960's he sang throughout the countries, fields, meadows, factories, hamlets, to be one with every tired and fatigued man of the world.

"It was a thrill to be able to introduce songs of Anglo-Americans and Americans to the hard-working people of that big city." He told about Calcutta in 1963. His songs, 'If I had a hammer,' ' Guantonamera', 'Where have all the flowers gone' remind me of Paul Robson. He is an ideal world citizen like John Lennon and Michael Jackson. He wrote and sang for coming men "Well the world may go/ when I am far away." The world needs an open society, free from every sort of intransigence and obscurantism, where no intellectual work shall be banned.

3

Last night I urinated blood. My friends in Chennai were tensed. They wanted to send me abroad for better treatment, but I needed to return to you all, to Calcutta. My knights are my children. I feel my end is knocking at the door. But I want to live for centuries to witness that greatest change of the world. Why did the providence give tortoise so long a life? What will it witness? What record will it prepare?

The 'Big Bang' theory states that creation of solar system is nothing but accidental. Universe or multiverse (if there is any) is the result of accident probably monitored and calculated by super conscious cosmos. Mankind should have been guided to focus attention beyond the Earth by astronomers, astrophysicists, prophets and philosophers. Man could have realized his supreme power, his originality, his importance, his unimportance. The elegance, colour, dignity of the universe, galaxies, stars, colourful nebula, clouds in the universe (factories of creation) supernova could have changed our mindset. At least a sea change would have been tangible. Physicists and astrophysicists should come out sometimes from their laboratories, the best temples of the world to guide mankind like Einstein and Stephen Hawking did.

"The kingdom of heaven is within." No wizard touch is needed for awakening. Self-touch is everything. You are your master. Each and every individual is his own master. So far, twentieth century is the worst century of our civilization for tremendous devastation. Even Einstein's best discovery was nastily misused. Poet Edwin Brock wrote:

These are, as I began, cumbersome ways
to kill a man. Simpler, direct, and much more neat
is to see that he is living somewhere in the middle
of the twentieth century, and leave him there.

We are born not to die only. We are born to know, to think, to work, to change, to create. If we can know the abysmal source of our creation we will think intensely. If we think intensely, we will change us, if we change ourselves, we can change the world and in that changed world we shall create a new world, a world altogether different from our present world.

My prostate condition is not satisfactory. I was taken to another oncologist for checkup. Dr Mill advised immediate operation. I did not dare. I don't want to go for any ordeal before my return to Calcutta. Dr Mill is on a mission to save cancer patients and has worked in some of the poor countries like Africa and Asia. He is a Chinese Christian. Dr Mill told, "Why some countries are poor? Because there are countries. Why there is religious fanaticism? Because there are religions" Actually, he is a non-believer and internationalist. He told directly, "If you undergo the operation you may not live longer. Now the choice is yours."

I am afraid we are not able to find remedies for Cancer. It is enveloping us like infernal cloud and patients die in excruciating pain and trauma. You all must take right measures to abolish this venomous disease from our ill administered planet. I covet a world where there is no cancer, no AIDS, no prostitution, no war, no terrorism, no environmental pollution and no bad politicians. These are equally detrimental in the creation of a graceful world civilization. We discovered Big Bang, Supernova, and we are discovering new galaxies every day. We even hope to get another solar system and solar family in the unending universe. But Cancer hasn't yet got any proper answer. I can only hope that our posterity will be successful in giving the internecine malady a permanent farewell. Man can do everything. We need time and patience. Definitely one of the important causes of this disease is pollution. Who will ask the government of US to stop poisoning the world? It is as good as global pollution. Costly machineries are manufactured in our countries and are exported just to kill men. The largest provider of defense servicing in India has a turnover of Rs 100 crore and it is hoped by the killer technologists that they would expand it to Rs 500 crores shortly. They say, "Servicing defense equipment locally is as important as producing it". But we fail to salvage a Cancer patient from inevitable collapse.

Soviet banditry is over. Waves of White House is swelling vehemently alongside its counterpart the terrorists. In every market place there is a butcher. So in shopkeeper's world there are terrorists. Cancer, AIDS, terrorism and ecological imbalance are products of the super competent *baniya*s. Even Bill Gates is one of the colossal '*dookander*', though he is a great figure. Rich countries' governments have changed their planet into garbage, it may cause ecological imbalance. Journeys of lives may once meet with inevitable collapse. Monumental personalities in various walks of life are rarefied. Man has got no creative slogan at least. Vulture salesmen are selling out flora and fauna and homosapiens' potentials. Shopkeepers and venders have discovered only one slogan in the world –

"SELL SELL & SELL
BUY BUY AND BUY"

Is it the death knell of our civilization? Certainly not. It is nothing but a phase of our history. Are we really living in a better world than the world of Huns and Tartars?

4

Have you ever heard of Kevin Carter, an internationally acclaimed photo journalist from South Africa? He was young when he committed suicide. In 1993 he went to photograph starving South Sudan. He took an iconic photo of starving little girl preyed upon by a vulture. After snapping the photograph, he chased away the vulture. Kevin was given Pulitzer Prize for that photograph. But he could not enjoy the prize for his biting conscience. In St Petersburg Time he was tremendously criticized. It wrote, "The man adjusting his lens to take just the right frame for her suffering might just as well be a predator, another vulture on the scene." Just in three months after the incident he committed suicide. In the suicide note he wrote, "I am depressed.... without phone... money for rent, money for child supports...money for debts.... money!!.... I am haunted by the vivid memories of killings and corpses and anger and pain.... of starving and wounded children, of trigger-happy mad men."

Another warning is looming large in accordance with Prof Stephen Hawking, of the phenomenal scientist. He warned, "The development of full artificial intelligence could spell the end of the human race." He further said, "It would take off on its own, and redesign itself at an ever-increasing rate. Humans, who are limited by slow biological evolution, couldn't compete and would be superseded." Elon Musk, chief executive of Rocket maker Space X is also afraid of 'AI'(Artificial Intelligence). He also warned that 'AI' is our biggest existential threat. But Prof Mark Bishop says key human abilities, such as understanding and consciousness are fundamentally lacking in so called 'intelligent computers.' But Steve Connor believes "It is one of our biggest existential threats, something so powerful and dangerous that it can put an end to the human race by replacing us with an army of intelligent robots." Long back in 1950, mathematician John Von Neumann talked of 'AI.'

Such things remind me of Charlie Chaplin's 'Modern Times'. He was one of the world's greatest futurologists. But even my dearest friend Charlie tried not to discover solution. No intelligence can supersede human intelligence because it is only Man who is capable of attaining spiritualism. Spiritualism is a quintessential part of human evolution. We have already wasted a long time despite arrival of Buddha, Jesus, Mir Kammal, Zarathustra, Nanak, Chaitanya, Sri Ramakrishna and many others. They did not come for creating a religious cult but they came for emancipation of mankind. It is Man who has created cults._Cult creation is a curse, creation of technology when put into positive use is a virtue. Very unintelligently Man has separated modern science, technology and spiritualism for his egotism and ego centric mindset.

Today Professor Hawking expresses his fear for A1(Artificial Intelligence). without any proper preparation to combat A1 we will be extinct. But there is something behind us to groom us up as supermen, to tackle and direct artificial intelligence easily, that is, super spiritual awakening. Jesus said, "I crossed seven gates to reach God and Heaven." These seven gates are latent in every man. And each man has got to cross those gates if he wants real enlightenment.

"Srinvantu viswe….. nanyah pantha vidyatehayanaya" Svetashara Upanishad 2/5,3/8

(O citizens of the world, listen, you are all from super truth, super eternity, the immortal masses from absolutism, listen, I have known that supra mental power and superior beloved, who is beyond dark and full with super light. If we know him we can cross the impediment of physical death. There is no other route to emancipation.)

'Aham brahmasmi' I am parambrahma, I am eternity (Brihadaranyak Upanishad)

Tomorrow's religions hopefully will go through evolution. Carl Sagan, the great scientist told, "A religion old or new that stressed the magnificence of the universe as revealed by modern science might be able to draw forth reserves of reverence and are hardly tapped by the conventional faith. Sooner or later such a religion will emerge." Sri Ramakrishna was a Kali worshipper, and had his divine supremacy in Christianity, Islam, Tantra and Vedanta. In future the world must follow his messages along with the messages of other prophets. To me Einstein, Newton and Marx were prophets of a different kind.

Al Qaida, Taliban and many other perverted organizations of the world in post-Cold War II are products of fighting superpowers. Any single country even the strongest one is too weak to run world administration alone. Any effort likewise will make worse mess than Hitler's ire on Jews. After abolition of Hitler, Mussolini and their compatriots, new sophisticated killers emerged. I feel like crying like a starving beggar in our country's street corner for creation of World Community. Probably I might die with that anxiety and that desire. Kashmir is burning, burning are the border zones of Israel and Arabia, Abyssinia, Congo, Nigeria, Sudan. Many other countries are panting in poverty, malaise and ill health. India does not dare help Pakistan's flood affected masses.

My Mother Earth is sicker than me, sicker than all the patients of the world. She is being raped by her children since the very dawn of civilization. Our real home is forgotten. Children! You have to dream big. None can shape your destiny, but your own selves. Nothing is beyond your reach. Only you are the makers of your destiny, destiny of your progeny, destiny of our planet.

5

I fell sick again and was shifted to Apollo for two weeks. All my students of 1984 batch have gone back to resume their work. My saviours are Dr Manipadam, Justice Kumar and Mrs Apparao. Nowadays I feel myself to be an extra burden for my Chennai friends and well-wishers. My life is in a state of 'no progression and no return.' I want to go back to my jail life again. Here I feel myself to be the most sophisticated prisoner of the world. Writing is my only solace, only respite.

But I am eagerly awaiting a new dawn, a magnificent dawn both for myself and the civilization. Our civilization has become severely infected with hatred, ambition, greed, bloodshed, massacre, genocide and so-called 'victories.'

Madam Apparao and Manipadam along with his friends are my usual companions now. My night nurse is healthy and robust. His name is also Ravi. He is a male nurse who always dreams of going to England. Still, I do not know who is funding my treatment and day to day expenditure. To me it is a Herculean expenditure. Dr Manipadam still dreams to create a new world with my direction and leadership. But I am a patient of carcinoma, a burden, a living…dead body.

Madam Apparao asked me many tough questions during our arguments. Sometimes I replied and sometimes she did it for me. One evening we both were sitting on the verandah. The sun was setting; tears trickled down her eyes. I did not know why, probably she was also not aware. We were discussing anti-Semitism. She asked me, "What is anti-Semitism?"

"Justifying Jew carnage and denying Jewish people's right to self-determination. Anti-Semitism is legal in many other countries. It claims that Jews killed Jesus. Hitler's Jew genocide in gas chambers had its supporters and accomplices. Accusing

Jew and Israel for exaggeration of holocaust. It is hostility towards the Jews because they are Jewish," I replied.

I explained to her how all kinds of hatred reached us from ancient times. Prophets and great souls have been coming to end the mess we have been making, and we have been discovering new mess after their departure. From ancient Greek and Roman periods anti-Semitism has been transferred to various civilizations from time to time. We gave it different shapes according to our frivolity, whims and caprices.

Madam Apparao told, "It was told that Gandhi was a naïve fool who tried in vain to sell his non-violence as panacea to the Nazi Fuehrer. According to some historians it was a faulty time for Mahatma to write to Hitler for pacification. Had Gandhiji been not busy with Indian Independence he would have started a peace crusade throughout the world. He could realize the dangerous outcome of the ensuing war. He gave Hitler Carte Blanche to decide. Definitely Gandhi knew Hitler would never be persuaded to relinquish his war romance, so in the first line of his first letter he wrote,

"Friends have been urging me to write to you for the sake of humanity."

"The Mahatma failed and we all will fail, because a massive chunk of humanity of the world does not know what human freedom is", returned Apparao.

"You are wrong." I replied.

"Humans of the world are lovers of their countries. They don't love the planet. They do not think about the total humanity nor do they love it", she told.

"Before arrival of Buddha, who knew Buddhism and before arrival of Jesus and Prophet Muhammad who knew Christianity and Islam? We have to knock at the very door of humankind's soul," I replied. I continued, "Human beings are most confused living beings since the very inception of civilization. We have been trying to work out a solution and unfortunately calculations are most of the time wrong. All the movements of our society need a strong linkage."

Cancer of civilization is in the second stage. At first stage stands two great wars and its malignant diplomacy. Weapons' discovery, weapon business and military research are viral and gradually becoming epidemical throughout the world. Present national and international systems are to be buried for creation of new man and new world. It is not possible till each and every individual understands or is taught about His great arrival and his importance and supremacy in the eternity and the universe. Remember the beautiful lines of "Twinkle Twinkle Little Star" of Jane Taylor, an English poet and novelist? This poem is known worldwide but authorship is forgotten. It was published in 1761 and was arranged by a number of famous composers including Mozart. Gone are those days of starry nights. Now space is a subject of parochial supremacy to the governments of US, China and Russia and many other countries. In 'Scientific American', a world-famous science Magazine of America, it is written "War in space may be closer than ever." More than 20,000 pieces of debris and space junk orbit around our planet.

I wrote several times every one is born with limitless power. But emperors, kings, dictators, rulers and governments (of many countries of the world) sometimes use that power diabolically. They are affected by the darkness of diabolic world. Men of the world! Will you now 'Shrink to your cellars, holes and cells?' Come out with your best weapon --- love, love and only love. Love your planet, love your fellowmen, love your sky, love your space, love your universe, and love your latent power of spiritual genre. If mankind does want to develop love for the planet and his own species, if he is ambitious enough to enjoy a world of peace, he has to try to unite the world of man and the earth per se for his own security and safety. Each and every man is supposed to resort to total unification at least to save our mother earth, its flora and fauna. COVID-19 Pandemic was a wake-up call for sure! We have other man-made dangers lurking too.

Great scientist APJ Abdul Kalam once quoted, "Within next few decades, we shall encounter a totally new situation of acute shortage of water, energy and minerals. No single nation will be able to handle the situation by itself. Humanity will require mega missions to harness solar energy, drinking water from sea through desalination and minerals from other planets. This will involve innovation and research in satellite based remote sensing of other planets, robotics, mining equipment, mining operations, extraction, beneficiations, processing and transportation."

It shall be well-nigh impossible if we are fragmented into nations, sects and classes. Dr Kalam still advised the youth, "Dream, dream and convert these into thoughts and actions..... think Big.... only then we can become big."

Everybody in the world feels there is a power, either in the Almighty or in Nature, or in the Universe. Theists, atheists, agnostics, monotheists, advaitists and dvaitaists feel it very intrinsically. We must have to leverage that feeling, that faith. Alexander Graham Bell, scientist, inventor, engineer and innovator who discovered telephone stated, "What this power is I cannot say. All I know is that it exists." The Upanishads quote, "This self is never born, nor does it die. It did not spring from anything, nor did anything spring from it. This ancient one is unborn, eternal, everlasting. It is not slain even though body is slain."

Again - "I am not, but the universe is myself."

There is no difference between the power of the universe and power of your atman. Both are same. After our cessation of ignorance, we can discover and feel that I and God are one. We need awareness, consciousness, super consciousness and action. Our universe is in perpetual cosmic speed and needs positive and constructive speed from its counterpart, that is 'you', that is 'we'. Dr Martin Luther King Jr. stated, "Take the first step in faith. You don't have to see the whole staircase."

Each of us is as great as the universe, but idiots do not know and as a result think and act negatively. James Ray stated, "Most people define themselves by this finite body but you are not a finite body. Even under a microscope you're an energy field. What we know about energy is this: you go to a quantum physicist and you say what creates the world? And he or she will say 'ENERGY'. Energy can never be created or destroyed. It always was, always has been, everything that ever existed always exists in its moving form.'

It resembles the magnificent tenets of the Upanishads and sermons of Swami Vivekananda. Everyone is the eternal energy. Everyone is a spiritual being. Our energy neither can be created nor destroyed. It changes form. We are the true kernel of us, the supreme energy of us has always been and always will be. 'We can never not be'. We are eternal, we are eternity. Each of us is that greatest and supermost light. Every man is spiritual, whether he agrees or not. So go ahead, unite humanity and let there be a great spiritual world. 'So aham'- I am that Power. 'Tatvam asi' – You are that Power. 'Aham brahmasmi' (Brihadaranyaka Upanishads)- I am Param Bramha, that great power. 'The core of my being is the ultimate reality, the roof and ground of the universe, the source that all exists. I am the reality.' You are that eternal light. You are that supramental power._Then why are we all fighting amongst ourselves to be the greatest?

6

From the hospital I was shifted to a rest house, that was more like a sophisticated imprisonment. But my men in Chennai had no choice. The rest house had a magnificent library and the knowledge shelves gave me tremendous hope.

"You cannot help the world by focusing on negative things. As you focus on the world's negative events, you not only add to them, but you also bring more negativity in your life. Pay attention to trust, love abundance, education and peace and do not think of world's problems," Rhonda Byrne had said. I do defer though – We have got to know the problems of the world if we crave for the greatest change in the system. Our unique positive thoughts can bring a new dawn. Every individual is the most powerful spiritual transmission tower of the universe.

We must try to make the universe accessible spiritually, to make our arrival phenomenal, and prepare mankind for the great cause for which he was born. It is high time to realise the latent power within oneself. If every individual can discover the power of the universe, evils of every kind shall be driven away giving rise to a spiritual awakening. We are not only born free but we are born with secret and latent spiritual enlightenment. We must discover that secret. We are the children of the universe, children of the Big Bang. I wish to discover that secret, not only for my own wisdom and progress, but for progress and gigantic advancement of man. Dr. John Hagelin had stated: "I see a future of unbounded potential, unbounded possibilities. Remember we are using, at most, 5% of the potential of the human mind, 100% human potential is result of proper education. Imagine a world where people are using their full mental and emotional potential. We could go anywhere, we could achieve anything." It is the most critical and exciting juncture in human history. In the greatest theatre of world civilization, we are the only participants, only actors, we have to perform with joy leaving aside the tension and nervousness.

Mahatma Gandhi had said, "Our armaments have piled already. Let us now be in search of something new; let us try the force of love and God which is truth." Professor Hawking said, "I don't think we will survive another 1000 years without escaping the fragile planet. I therefore want to encourage public interest in space." He had stated that AI (Artificial Intelligence) would expedite our demise, for improvement of technology and machinery might overpower human race. I believe AI fear is not an intelligent fear. Emotionless, unromantic artificial intelligence shall always be overruled by man. I am highly optimistic about future of humans and Earth.

According to Dalai Lama, violence is a 20th century phenomenon. When he was asked about the role of Artificial Intelligence and human being, he was very optimistic of human intelligence. Dalai Lama expected all 7 billion people of the world should love each other instead of expressing hostility. He said: "Evil is man's own creation and man has the ability to overcome these hindrances." He expressed his concern over children's starvation in Yemen. Dalai Lama is a harbinger of Ahimsa or non-violence. I too believe global non-violent movement for unification of man. It is an integral part of human evolution. Even Greek philosopher Aristotle expressed his frustration for man. But I am not frustrated, we have to change our mindset and we shall surely succeed in our mission.

I am now a dying patient. I convinced my friends to allow me to go to Calcutta. During this long span whatever I wrote, I wrote it in pain and shock. Some of my friends decided to accompany me by train for the doctor prohibited air travel. The time finally came for me to leave and head home. One fine morning we with all our belongings reached the station. I was not feeling too good and was out of breath. Madam Apparao and Mantri immediately stood beside me and held my hands. On the platform the GRP were all around me. Piramanyangam being an IPS officer took the risk of escorting me. It was dawn and the sky was dark, overcast with clouds. It was a cool Deccan winter morning. The train slowly started leaving the station. Dr Manipadam along with his family and Dr Abraham came to see me off. As the train gathered speed, they were all left behind.

Aditya said, "I have informed all your well-wishers and friends that you are returning."

As the train sped, I thought whether mankind would unite if there was an attack from another planet or planets! But I wish it did. When COVID-19 had first attacked mankind all over the world, I developed a thin faith of world unification against the malady. But it failed, though Covid 19 with all its mutants is the super enemy of the entire human race. Vaccines are being improved every day for the maximum benefit. We have to stop glorifying war and henceforth try to glorify the essence of unity in mankind.

Its night, the outside is dark like a ghost's den. Our train is running, breaking through the dark silence. My personality has undergone a transformation. The fire in me is still incandescent. I am desirous of spiritual purification and joy. The train reached a station. It was quite empty and quiet. It was almost 2am. I came to my friends in the compartment. They all lay fast asleep. I am again in a confusion with my life. In Calcutta my life shall be colourless, dull and unchequered. I shall have to pay more attention to my various maladies. Should I then leave my friends in the train and run in my own direction? I came back to my seat and tried to meditate. I have not been meditating since my prison days. I recited:

"ka taba kanta/ Kaste putra, samsar ebo ati bichitra, kasya mata, kasya pita/
kasya bhrata sahadarya, ka pranena sambadha, kakasya paribedana"

Adi Sankaracharya felt this after prolonged penance. It roughly translates to who is your wife, who is your son, the world is very surprising. Who is your mother? Who is your father? Where is your brother? Human body gets connected to *atma*, for whom should we repent? Atma, the great soul of man is always free from worldly bondage. In our world, sometimes I am Sunder and sometimes I am Satarup Goswamy. Piramanayangam was already influenced practically, which, in fact, made everything disappointing. A curtain window of the train is open, the sound of an instrument comes wafting by.

Oh! Lift me as a wave, a leaf, a cloud!

I fall upon **the thorns of life**! I bleed!

My return to Calcutta will give me another incarceration. My soul is never too old. I can again travel and shake the world around me despite my physical frailty. If my life ends without any spiritual power and contribution without guidance to know thyself and if I return, I shall have to face a dull and meaningless life.

How dull it is to pause, to make an end,
To rust unburnish'd, not to shine in use!
As tho' to breathe were life! Life piled on life
Were all too little, and of one to me
Little remains: but every hour is saved
From that eternal silence, something more,
A bringer of new things; and vile it were
For some three suns to store and hoard myself,
And this gray spirit yearning in desire
To follow knowledge like a sinking star,

I would like to be enlightened by wisdom to enlighten the world for my progeny. After World War I in 1918, people of the world had had great negativity. It was another monolithic virus to develop inertia in man, like that of today. Super inertia recoiled men of the world like octopus as Covid 19 did a century later. Some 71 years ago, George Orwell wrote his book "Nineteen Eighty four," where he referred to a cataclysmic condition of the world. Many ugly sights and scenes were alluded by him. Today's pandemic resembles the prediction of George Orwell.

'Live and let Live.' Who are financing and patronising the terrorists throughout the world? Students and young men have to stand boldly against this man-made chaos for centuries together. The world needs another Emperor Ashoka and universities like Nalanda, Taxila and Vikramshila. Swami Vivekananda had said: "Religion is a science, as study is the greatest and healthiest exercise the human mind can have." Students, young men! Earn spiritual power. It is our world. It is just not the legacy of governments and the rich. It is legacy of human race till the last moment of the civilization. Without Global Peace Revolution, nothing will improve. Some Satanic persons always try to create their own lobbies of puppet governments, parallel mafia governments and warlords for destruction. Go to your rooftop at midnight and look at the sky. What do the million stars signify? What do they want to say? Messages from the Almighty are written round about the Earth, the world, the sun, the moon, the Earth is always giving us messages. Universal messages are never written on stone plates. It is dynamically rampant even in the tiniest and exiguous particles of dust. We are all "Amritasya Putra," the brightest children and carriers of light.

After a long time, I realised that I have been contemplating for the last few hours. This time the seating arrangement in the train compartment was scattered. I was really unmindful on seeing a group of paramilitary force loitering in our compartment and felt puzzled. Madam Apparao came with Debasis Mantri and Aditya. We had a long chat. Madam Apparao looked very anxious. One of the paramilitary personnel came to me directly and asked my name, my whereabouts etc. It was night time. We all retired for the night. I started dreaming. I saw the nocturnal sky covered with stars. After a short while I saw millions of stars swimming in the dark blue sky. A melodious music could be heard. Oh! What a beautiful feeling! What a harmony! A blue star was coming towards me and was gradually becoming bigger. It enveloped me completely. I felt cool and calm. A celestial fragrance was all around me. I was enjoying every moment of the heavenly bliss.

Suddenly, I woke up from sleep. But I was still enveloped in the same beauty, aroma and symphony. I could still see the star. The train had stopped at a platform. I did not know the name.

In fact, since the beginning of my arrest, I was probably believed by the intelligence department to be Satarup Goswamy, the surreptitious terrorised Naxal leader. Though I was released with joy and ecstasy, I was never believed by the entire administration of my non-involvement with Naxalites. I was watched secretly by the Government of South India. On my way to Calcutta, I understood that I was not really a freeman.

All of a sudden, a paramilitary force approached me and asked for my name. I knew Pira had no choice. I surmised that I might be incarcerated again. I took permission to go to the toilet. They allowed, and I jumped out of my compartment, and so did Aditya. I started running, and four or five paramilitary personnel were chasing me. I could hear them shouting, "*Ruk jao.*" I did not pay any heed. I was running at a breakneck speed. There was a chanting of hymns coming from somewhere.

There was a sound behind me. Aditya called out. He had fallen down. The paramilitary personnel warned out loudly.

They asked me to stop or they would shoot. I did not stop. I could see the star before me. I could not stop now, I had to reach to it. I felt a piercing pain in my left leg. I realised they had actually fired. I could not run anymore. I fell down. The star was slowly retreating. It was moving away. There was another shot. A bullet penetrated my right arm. A numbness enveloped me. I could not feel any pain. I felt the light of the bright blue star lifting me up. A feeling of slumber engulfed me, enfolding me, slowly....

"Goswamy halt, halt…"

I could hear the military men asking me to halt. But I could not halt!

vive vive vive la man
vive la mother earth
Feeling so calm and peaceful...
A bullet pierced through my left thigh,
I fell down, blood
Was gushing out profusely.
Excruciating pain!
Meanwhile, I was cordoned
Off by those armed personnel.
I screamed at them
Haphazardly to allow me to
Finish my writing.
They allowed.
Now I have nothing to
Write being awfully handicapped.
I have written everything
I felt and dreamt.
I am a prisoner again.
Children, please hand over this
Diary to my Henrietta.
Good bye
Jay Ramakrishna.